Canadian Mapping Big Book

Grades 1-3

Written by Lynda Golletz
Illustrated by S&S Learning Materials

About the Author:
Lynda Golletz was an elementary school teacher for thirty-three years. She is the author of many educational resources for teachers and students. Ms Golletz has travelled across Canada several times.

ISBN 978-1-55495-028-7
Copyright 2009

Published in Canada by:
S&S Learning Materials
15 Dairy Avenue
Napanee, Ontario
K7R 1M4
www.sslearning.com

At A Glance - Grades 1 to 2

Learning Expectations	Canada's Shape and Location on Globes	Canada's Shape and Location on Maps	Symbols, Legends, Scale, Directions, Colour, Grids	Mapping Rooms and Parks	Games, Word Scramble, Word Sort	Mapping Schoolyard	Mapping School Neighbourhood	Many Kinds of Maps	Water Words, Word Sort and Country, Province, Territory
Understanding Concepts									
• Recognize that the world is made up of countries, continents, and regions.	•	•	•					•	
• Recognize Canada as part of North America.	•	•	•					•	
• Identify a variety of maps and locate Canada on them.	•	•	•					•	
• Identify earth as a sphere, half the earth as a hemisphere, and demonstrate an understanding that the globe is a model of the earth.	•		•						
• Recognize that maps represent real places.	•	•		•		•	•	•	•
Map and Globe Skills									
• Make and read concrete, pictorial, and simple maps to locate information.			•	•		•	•	•	•
• Use appropriate map vocabulary.	•		•	•	•	•	•	•	•
• Recognize and use pictorial symbols, colour, legends, keys, and cardinal directions on maps of Canada.		•	•						
• Use non standard units to measure distance on a map.		•							
• Use their own symbols on a map.				•	•	•	•		
• Recognize the major parallels of latitude.	•	•			•			•	
• Recognize that different colours represent different things on maps.	•	•	•	•		•	•		•
• Make and read maps of familiar areas in their local community.			•			•	•	•	
Inquiry/Research Communication Skills									
• Use maps to locate information about their own community.	•	•	•				•	•	
• Make and read maps of their local community.			•	•		•	•		
• Sort and classify information obtained from maps.	•							•	•
• Read a variety of maps to obtain information.	•	•	•					•	•

At A Glance - Grade 3

Learning Expectations	Canada's Shape and Location on Globes and Many Maps	Many Kinds of Maps	Symbols, Legends, Scale, Directions, Colour, Grids	Continents, provinces and territories	Games, Word Sort	Mapping Kitchen and Aquaplex	Canada's Landforms and Oceans	Urban and Rural Communities	Water Words, Word Sort
Understanding Concepts									
• Recognize that the world is made up of countries, continents and regions	●	●	●	●				●	
• Recognize Canada as part of North America	●	●	●	●				●	
• Identify a variety of maps and locate Canada on them	●	●	●	●				●	
• Identify a variety of maps and their uses	●	●	●	●					
• Identify earth as a sphere, half the earth as a hemisphere, and demonstrate an understanding that the globe is a model of the earth	●	●							
• Recognize that maps represent real places	●	●		●		●	●	●	●
Map and Globe Skills									
• Make and read pictorial and simple maps to locate information	●	●	●	●		●	●	●	●
• Recognize and use pictorial symbols, colour, legends, keys, and cardinal and intermediate directions on maps of Canada	●	●	●	●	●		●		
• Use standard units to measure distance on a map (scale)			●						
• Use own symbols on a map			●	●		●			
• Recognize the major parallels of latitude	●	●	●		●				
• Recognize the major meridians of longitude	●	●	●						
• Recognize that different colours represent different things on maps	●	●	●	●		●	●		●
• Make and read maps of familiar areas in their own environment			●			●		●	
• Locate Canada's provinces and territories					●		●		
• Identify major landforms of Canada							●		
• Locate oceans near Canada							●		
Inquiry/Research Communication Skills									
• Recognize urban and rural communities		●						●	
• Use maps to locate information about their own community and provinces and territories	●	●	●	●			●	●	●
• Compare provinces and territories	●	●		●			●		
• Make and read maps of their local community		●	●					●	●
• Sort and classify information obtained from maps	●	●	●	●	●		●	●	●
• Read a variety of maps to obtain information	●	●		●			●	●	●

Table of Contents - Grades 1 to 2

CANADA'S SHAPE AND LOCATION

CANADA MAPS AND MAP FEATURES

Table of Contents - Grades 1 to 2

Table of Contents - Grade 3

Table of Contents - Grade 3

CANADA'S PROVINCES AND TERRITORIES

MAJOR LANDFORMS AND BODIES OF WATER IN CANADA

CANADIAN COMMUNITIES – URBAN AND RURAL

Teacher Rubric Canadian Mapping - Grades 1 to 2

Student's Name: _____ Date: _____

Criteria	Level 1	Level 2	Level 3	Level 4
Can recognize the shape of Canada on a variety of maps.	Not at all	Just on a basic map	On a variety of maps in usual orientation	On a variety of maps and in a variety of orientations
Demonstrates knowledge of Canada within North America.	Not at all	Just on a basic map	On a variety of maps in usual orientation	On a variety of maps and in a variety of orientations
Demonstrates knowledge of maps as representing real places.	Little evidence	Some evidence	Good evidence	Excellent evidence
Identifies earth as a sphere, half the earth as a hemisphere, and demonstrates an understanding that the globe is a model of the earth.	Not at all	Some evidence	Good evidence	Excellent evidence
Makes and reads simple maps to locate information.	Much difficulty	Can with a great deal of assistance	Can with a little assistance	Excellent and with almost no assistance
Uses appropriate map vocabulary.	Little evidence	Some evidence	Good	Excellent
Recognizes and uses pictorial symbols, colour, legends, keys, and cardinal directions on maps of Canada.	Little competency	Some competency	Satisfactory competency	Excellent competency
Makes and reads maps of their local community.	Little competency	Some competency	Satisfactory competency	Excellent competency
Locates local community on a map of Canada.	Not at all	Some competency with assistance	Some competency with a little assistance	Excellent competency

Teacher Rubric Canadian Mapping - Grade 3

Student's Name: _____ Date: _____

Criteria	Level 1	Level 2	Level 3	Level 4
Can recognize the shape of Canada on a variety of maps.	Not at all	Just on basic map	On a variety of maps if usual orientation	On a variety of maps and in a variety of orientations
Demonstrates knowledge of Canada within North America.	Not at all	Just on basic map	On a variety of maps if usual orientation	On a variety of maps and in a variety of orientations
Demonstrates knowledge of maps as representing real places.	Little evidence	Some evidence	Good evidence	Excellent evidence
Names and locates Canada's provinces and territories.	Not at all	Some evidence	Good evidence	Excellent evidence
Identifies earth as a sphere, half the earth as a hemisphere, and demonstrates an understanding that the globe is a model of the earth.	Not at all	Some evidence	Good evidence	Excellent evidence
Locates equator, prime meridian, and major parallels of latitude.	Much difficulty	Can with a great deal of assistance	Can with a little assistance	Excellent and with almost no assistance
Makes and reads simple maps to locate information.	Much difficulty	Can with a great deal of assistance	Can with a little assistance	Excellent and with almost no assistance
Uses appropriate map vocabulary.	Little evidence	Some evidence	Good	Excellent
Recognizes and uses pictorial symbols, colour, legends, keys, and cardinal and intermediate directions on maps of Canada.	Little competency	Some competency	Satisfactory competency	Excellent competency
Locates local community on a map of Canada.	Not at all	Some competency with assistance	Some competency with a little assistance	Excellent competency
Identifies urban and rural locations and can site their differences.	Not at all	Some competency with assistance	Some competency with a little assistance	Excellent competency
Identifies the continents.	Not at all	Some competency with assistance	Some competency with a little assistance	Excellent competency

Student Self-Assessment Rubric

Name: _____   Date: _____

In the box, draw the face that best describes your performance. Then, add your points to determine your total score.

Expectations	Needs Improvement (1 point) ☹	Sometimes (2 points) 😐	Always/ almost always (3 points) ☺	My Points
I can find Canada on many maps.				
I can find places on a Canada map.				
I can draw symbols.				
I can make tidy maps.				
I can use a map legend/key.				
I colour and label maps well.				
I can use the map scale.				
I can follow the Compass Rose directions.				
I can name three or more maps and their uses.				

Introduction

The activities in "Canadian Mapping Grades 1 to 3" closely follow the expectations outlined in the curricula of the provinces and territories of Canada. They have been designed to provide a variety of mapping experiences, appealing to a range of learning styles.

Teacher Preparations

1. **Equipment Needed:** It is recommended that teachers gather the following resources to use with Canadian Mapping: a large wall map of the world, a large wall map of North America, a large wall map of Canada, a globe, road maps, books appropriate to Grades Two and Three pertaining to mapping, an overhead projector, and maps of the local community and a map of the school (indoors and outside).

2. Label the classroom with the cardinal and intermediate directions placed on the corresponding walls of the classroom.

Maps: Students will enjoy bringing maps to school from home and sharing these with the class. Encourage comparisons and decide upon uses of maps. Many schools have old maps in storage. Students will enjoy comparing these to newer maps. A "Map Morning" could be held. Adult volunteers could work with small groups to examine various Canadian maps (e.g. Canada maps, road maps, and tourist maps). Groups could periodically rotate from map to map. Focus should be on the use of a map, Legend/Key, map scale, and directions. This could be followed-up by a map-making activity with adult volunteers assisting.

Teacher Information

What is a Map?

A map is a drawn or printed representation of the earth or any other heavenly body. Most maps are flat, although some have raised surfaces. A globe is also a map in the shape of a sphere.

Maps provide information through lines, colours, shapes, and symbols. The symbols represent such features as rivers, lakes, roads, and cities. The features on a map are greatly reduced in size. The distance of 160 kilometres (100 miles) might be represented by 2.5 centimetres (1 inch) on a map.

Maps are used to locate places, measure distances, plan trips, and find our way. Pilots of ships and airplanes use maps to navigate. Maps provide us with information about a place such as climate, population, and transportation routes. Some maps show such patterns as where people live and how they use the land.

Through the years, people have explored more of the world and have added new information to maps. Scientific discoveries have made maps more accurate. Today, most maps are based on photographs taken from the air. The making and study of maps is called cartography. The maker of a map, or someone who studies maps is called a cartographer.

Types of Maps

There are many types of maps. The most common ones are **general reference maps, mobility maps, thematic maps,** and **inventory maps.**

General reference maps identify and locate various geographic features. They may include land features, bodies of water, political boundaries, cities and towns, roads, and many other elements. General reference maps are used to locate specific places and to observe their location in relation to other places. Examples of general reference maps are maps of provinces, states, countries, and continents. These maps are usually found in atlases.

A **political map** is one that emphasizes the boundaries of counties, provinces, states and countries.

Physical maps or terrain maps emphasize the location of physical features found on the earth's surface such as mountains, rivers and lakes.

Mobility maps are created to help people find their way from one place to another. There are mobility maps for travel on land, on water or in the air. Maps that are used to navigate ships and planes are called charts.

The most common mobility map is a road map. A **road map** represents different types of roads such as divided highways, four-lane roads, major routes and scenic routes. It also shows the location of cities, towns, provincial and state parks, and other places connected by these roads. Travellers use road maps to plan trips and to follow lengthy routes. A **street map** is similar to a road map. It shows a much smaller area in much greater detail. This type of map is used to locate specific addresses and to plan and follow short routes.

Transit maps show the routes of buses, subways, and other systems of public transportation in cities and towns. These maps help people reach their destination by means of public transportation.

Aeronautical charts are maps used to navigate airplanes. Pilots of small, low-flying aircraft plan and follow a course by using VFR charts (visual flight rules charts). VFR charts show landmarks as bridges, highways, railroad tracks, rivers, and towns. These charts also show the location of airports, the heights of mountains, and other obstructions. Pilots of low-flying airplanes and crews of high-flying aircraft use IFR charts (instrumental flight rules charts). These charts are designed for radio navigation. IFR charts locate transmitters that beam very high radio frequency signals, which help pilots and airplane crews to determine their position and course.

Nautical charts are maps used to navigate ships and boats. They show the depths of water, the location of lighthouses, buoys, islands, and dangers such as coral reefs and underwater mountains that come close to the surface. Nautical charts also locate the source of radio signals that navigators use to determine their course and position.

Thematic Maps

A **thematic map** shows the distribution of a particular feature such as population, rainfall or a natural resource. This type of map is used to study an overall pattern. A thematic map may show where wheat is produced in North America or how the average rainfall varies from one part of a country to another. Quantities are expressed on thematic maps through the use of symbols or colours.

Inventory Maps

Inventory maps are similar to thematic maps in the way that they concentrate on a specific feature. These maps show the precise location of the specific feature. A map showing every building in a community is an example of an inventory map.

GIS: GIS is a mapping system that uses computers to collect, store, manipulate, analyze, and display data.

Satellite Images: Satellite images are photos taken of earth by robotic devices positioned in satellites. They show various sections of the earth and have many uses. They are used in weather prediction.

Reading a Map

In order to read a map, one must understand map legends, scale, geographic grids, and map indexes. A map legend lists and explains the symbols and colours found on a map. Sometimes the map symbols do resemble the features that they represent. For example, a tree-shaped symbol may represent a forest or an orchard. Many symbols have no resemblance to what they represent at all. For example, a circle or large dot may represent where a city stands or it may represent where a group of homes can be found. It is very important to read the map legend to find out what the symbols mean. Most maps are printed to show north at the top. Most map legends include an arrow that indicates which direction is north.

Scale

The scale on a map shows the relationship between distances on the map and the corresponding distances on the earth's surface. Scale is shown on a straight line with distances marked off on a bar scale. A bar scale is like a ruler or measuring tape. You can measure long distances with a bar scale. Each mark represents a certain number of kilometres or miles.

Some maps indicate scale in words and figures. The scale might appear as 2.5 centimetres – 10 kilometres (1 inch = 6 miles). In other words, 2.5 centimetres (1 inch) represents a distance of 10 kilometres (6 miles) on the earth's surface.

Geographic Grids

Geographic grids are lines on maps that help us find and describe locations. The most common grid uses the east-west lines, called **parallels**, and the north-south lines, called **meridians**. The parallel lines and the meridians form the **graticule**.

Parallels are lines that encircle the globe from east to west. The parallel that lies exactly halfway between the North and South Pole is called the **equator**. **Parallels** are used to measure **latitude**. They measure distance from the equator toward either pole. Latitude is measured in degrees of a circle. Any point on the equator has a latitude of zero degrees, written 0°. The North Pole has a latitude of 90° north and the South Pole has a latitude of 90° south. Parallels are sometimes called the lines of latitude.

Meridians are lines that extend halfway around the globe from the North Pole to the South Pole. Mapmakers count meridians from the line that passes through Greenwich, England, a borough of London. The Greenwich meridian is also known as the **prime meridian**. Meridians measure longitude, which is the distance east or west of the prime meridian. **Longitude** is measured in degrees of a circle too. Meridians run from 0° at Greenwich to 180°. The 180° meridian lies halfway around the world from the Prime Meridian. Meridians are sometimes called lines of longitude.

Longitude and latitude are used to pinpoint places around the world.

Map Indexes

A **map index** helps us to locate places on a map. The features shown on a map are listed in alphabetical order in the index. At the back of most atlases, an index is found. Each entry in the index is listed with its longitude and latitude.

Some maps are divided into horizontal rows and vertical columns by an index grid. Letters are often used along the sides of the map to label the horizontal lines. Numbers are used across the top and bottom of the map to label the vertical rows. In this case, each entry in the map index is followed by a letter and a number corresponding to a row and a column on the map. This feature is found where the row and column cross.

Hemispheres

A **hemisphere** is one-half of a sphere. The word hemisphere is the name given to any half of the globe. It comes from the Greek word that means "half a sphere." The world is divided into four main hemispheres. They are 1) the northern and southern hemispheres, 2) the eastern and western hemispheres, 3) land and water hemispheres, and 4) daylight and darkness hemispheres.

The northern and southern hemispheres share the equator as a boundary line. All areas north of the equator make up the northern hemisphere. All areas south of the equator make up the southern hemisphere.

The eastern and western hemispheres have no natural dividing line such as the equator. The eastern hemisphere, or "Old World," is made up of the continents of Europe, Asia, Africa, and Australia. The western hemisphere or "New World" is made up of the continents of North America and South America.

The earth is also divided as a land hemisphere and a water hemisphere. The land hemisphere includes the half of the earth with the most land. Its centre lies near London, England. The other half of the earth is mostly water and makes up the water hemisphere. Its centre lies near New Zealand.

During a day, one half of the earth is in darkness and the other is in light. The earth is also separated into daylight and darkness hemispheres. There is no sharp boundary between the daylight and darkness hemispheres. They are separated by the twilight zones of dawn and dusk. At the same time, they are continually changing position on the surface of the earth as it rotates on its axis.

Directional Indicators

Most maps have a symbol called a **Compass Rose**. The purpose of the Compass Rose is to show the cardinal directions: North, South, East, West. Some Compass Roses have only four lines, called "petals." Some directional indicators may only have "N" for North.

Sometimes a Compass Rose will have more than four directions. These are called the intermediate directions. The intermediate petals fall between two of the cardinal directions. They are called northeast, southeast, northwest, and southwest. One way to remember directions is with the word "WE": West is on the left and East is on the right.

If a Compass Rose is not found on the map, the top of the map is usually north.

Map Symbols

One way to show features on a map is to create symbols that represent them. A symbol is a shape or pattern that represents an object. Symbols and their meanings are shown on a key or legend on the map.

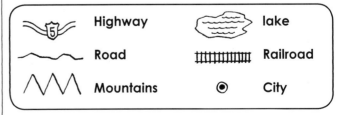

Glossary of Geographic Terms

Aerial Photo: photographs of terrain on the ground taken by cameras mounted in aircraft

Antarctic Circle: an imaginary line of latitude 66° 30 (66 degrees 30 minutes) south of the equator

Arctic Circle: an imaginary line of latitude 66° 30' north of the equator

Atlantic Provinces: Newfoundland and Labrador, New Brunswick, Nova Scotia, Prince Edward Island are the Atlantic provinces of Canada

Bay: a part of an ocean, sea or lake extending into land

Basin: a depression or hollow which may or may not contain water; surrounded by higher land

Bird's-eye view: a location or topic as if viewed from an altitude or distance above

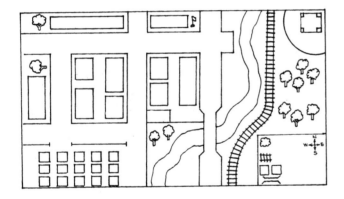

Border: often called political border, the official line separating two countries or provinces or territories

Canadian Shield: an area of Precambrian rock that underlies almost half of Canada

Capital City: a city that is the official seat of government for that province, territory or Canada

Cardinal directions: the four compass directions – north, south, east, west – which are read along the meridians and parallels on the globe.

City: an important or large municipality, usually having a larger population than a town, village or borough.

Community: a specific locality including those who live there

Compass Rose: the design, which shows the directions on a map; the north and south "petals" are usually longer than the east, west and intermediate "petals."

Continent: largest landmasses on Earth. i.e. North America, South America, Europe, Asia, Africa, Australia, Africa, Antarctica

Cordilleras: a chain of mountains, especially the principal mountain system of a continent such as Rocky Mountains in North America

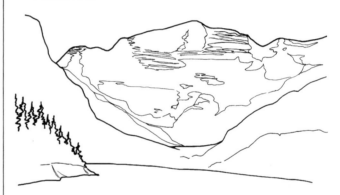

Country: an area of land on earth that has a government

Degree: one of the 360 units of measurement that make up a circle, represented by the symbol °. Degrees are subdivided into 60 minutes, represented by the symbol .

East: the direction along a parallel toward the rising sun

Eastern hemisphere: the half of the earth that includes Africa, Asia, Australia, Europe, and their waters.

Equator: an imaginary line of latitude (0°) halfway between the North and South Poles.

Globe: the only true world map, made on a ball or sphere the shape of the earth.

Grid: the network of meridians and parallels on a map

Gulf: an area of water bordering on and lying within a curved coastline, usually larger than a bay and smaller than a sea; sometimes nearly surrounded by land

Harbour: a sheltered body of water where ships anchor and are safe from the winds and waves of storms at sea.

Hemisphere: any half of the earth's surface

Intermediate Directions: directions between the cardinal directions: northeast, northwest, southeast and southwest

Island: an area of land surrounded by water.

Key: the part of a map that explains what the symbols on the map mean (also called a legend).

Label: a word on a map indentifying the location.

Lake: a body of fresh or salt water entirely surrounded by land

Land: the portion of the earth's surface above the level of the sea or ocean

Landforms: natural features of the earth's surface

Latitude: the distance, measured in degrees, north or south of the equator

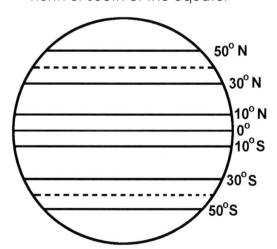

Legend: the part of a map that explains what the symbols on the map mean(also called a key).

Longitude: imaginary lines that run from the North Pole to the South Pole. They measure distances east and west of the prime meridian. Lines of longitude are sometimes referred to as meridians.

Maritime Provinces: New Brunswick, Nova Scotia, Prince Edward Island; provinces of Canada

Mountain: a lofty elevation on the earth's surface

Map: a drawing of all or part of the earth

North: the directions along a meridian toward the North Pole and the North Star.

North Pole: the point farthest north on the earth's surface. It is 90° north of the equator.

Northern Hemisphere: the half of the earth's surface north of the equator

Ocean: one of the large areas of the earth into which the water surface is divided

Parallel: a latitude line running east and west around the earth parallel to the equator

Plain (prairies): a flat or level area of land

Physical map: a map that emphasizes land elevation and major physical features

Political map: a map that emphasizes countries, states, provinces, territories, and cities

Prairie: any natural grassland; usually used to describe vast areas of level or rolling land without trees

Prairie Provinces: Alberta, Saskatchewan, Manitoba, provinces of Canada

Prime Meridian: the zero meridian from which east and west longitude are measured, passing through London (Greenwich)

Province: part of a country; Canada is a country with ten provinces and three territories

Region: part of the earth that shares similar characteristics

River: a large stream of water which flows on the earth's surface

Rural: a country setting, usually with many farms and small settlements

Satellite Image: photos taken by robotic devices positioned in satellites and transmitted to earth

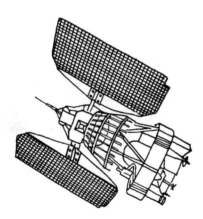

Scale: the numerical relationship between an actual distance on the earth and the distance which represents it on a map

Sea: a large body of salt water smaller than an ocean

Sound: a long and rather narrow body of water, larger than a strait; connecting two large bodies of water or separating a large island from the mainland

South: the directions along a meridian toward the South Pole

South Pole: the point farthest south on the earth's surface. It is 90° south of the equator.

Southern Hemisphere: the half of the earth's surface south of the equator

Symbol: a drawing, letter or figure that represents a feature or idea

Strait: a narrow body of water connecting two larger bodies of water

Territory: part of a country; Canada is a country with ten provinces and three territories

Town: a community of people ranging from a few hundred to several thousand; larger than a village, but smaller than a city

Urban: a city or town with many buildings and streets

Valley: a long, narrow land area lying between two areas of higher elevation. A valley usually contains a river or stream.

Village: a small group of houses and other buildings in a rural area ranking in size between a hamlet and a town

West: the direction along a parallel toward the setting sun

Western Hemisphere: the half of the earth that includes North America, South America and their waters

World Map: a map depicting all of the land masses and oceans of the world

Helpful Teacher Notes for Specific Pages - Grades 1 to 2:

Pages 19, 20, 21: Colouring Maps

It is well worth the time taken to insist early on that map colouring and labelling guidelines be followed. Explain that a map is intended to provide us with information. It must be legible.

- Colour inside the lines using horizontal movements.
- Colours should not mix.
- Shade lightly.
- Label in small, neat printing.
- Label rivers by printing along the meandering direction of the river.
- All maps should have great titles that immediately tell us how this map will be useful.
- The best maps include a Legend or Key.

Page 24: My Canada Puzzle

It will be important to demonstrate this technique before students begin. On the chalkboard, show a few versions. Point out that most of the lines go directly to the edge of the map.

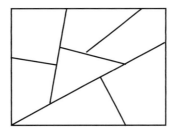

Page 25: Canada From Space

Explain that a satellite is something that travels around the planet Earth. It can be an artificial platform placed into orbit around the earth, often carrying instruments to gather environmental data. Be sure to mention to students that an artist has added the white outline to the satellite image to help them see the shape of the land.

Page 27: A Globe

As your students observe, take some photos of your classroom globe from above and below. Provide time for students to look at these photos and discuss them.

Page 29: A Globe is a Sphere

As your students observe, cut an orange into two sections to depict the Northern and Southern hemispheres. Cut a second orange to depict the Eastern and Western hemispheres.

Page 30: Globe Puzzle

Be sure to show on a real globe the Northern hemisphere (looking down from above).

Pages 34, 35: Mapping Canada

If possible, show the students real examples of these maps, locating Canada on each.

Pages 38, 39, 40: Map a Room

Model this activity by drawing with student input a map of the classroom. Include a Legend or Key.

Pages 44, 45: Compass Rose: Directions North, South, East, West
The gymnasium is a great place to play games to review directions. Label the gym walls North, South, East, and West. For example: Blindfold a student. Have a second student lead him/her from point A to point B via oral directions using the N, S, E, and W directions. Keep the path simple, with safety of prime importance.

Page 55: Using a Grid Map
If possible, show your students real maps with grids.

Page 60: Find the Equator and the Poles on a Globe
A teacher named Rebecca suggested this kinaesthetic activity on <u>about.com Geography</u>.

Page 62: Many Many Maps
If possible, show the students real examples of these maps, locating Canada on each.

Page 63: Global Views
Use the real globe and the photos you have taken of it to show the various views.

Page 65: Canada's Water
Describe the river systems in Canada as being similar to a tree. Draw samples on the board. Use terms source, mouth, branch, tributary, river, stream, delta, etc. It is recommended that students wear "paint shirts" over their clothing. Once the water systems are dry and labelled, provide time for students to circulate to see the other river systems in the room and point out that this is how it is with the real river systems of Canada. Each is different, but with the same components.

Page 68: A Canadian Community
Be sure to discuss why we don't put moving objects on maps.

Page 69: Where I Live
Students will need assistance with locating and spelling the name of their locale.

Page 71: Lindsay and Anil's Canadian Community
This activity could be extended. Ask students to print the numbers 1 to 8 in the correct places on the map.

Page 72: A Walk in Our School Neighbourhood
Be sure to take along some adult helpers. The students will need assistance with reading the items on the list. When you are in the schoolyard and in the community, point out the directions and relate them to real places they will know. For example: "Turn and face East. Look towards McCready's store. That is East."

Page 73: A Map of Our Schoolyard
Provide students with an outline map of the yard and the shape of the school already on it.

Pages 77, 78: Assessment One and Two:
These are read aloud to the students. They respond by colouring on their individual sheets. Collect and mark.

Canada in North America

Canada is part of the continent called North America.

Colour all of the water on this map blue.

Colour Canada red.

Colour the other countries green.

Cut out this label and paste it on the map.

Canada

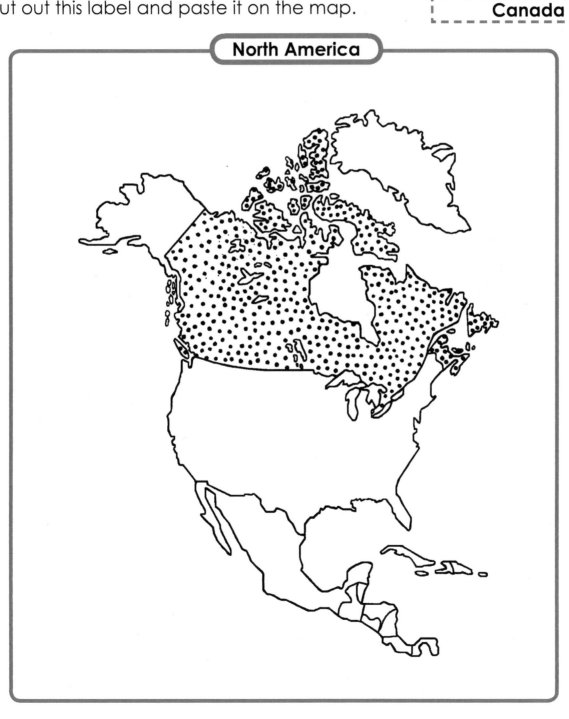

North America

CANADIAN MAPPING

Our Country Canada

Trace around the shape of our country Canada.

Trace the name of our country Canada.

Colour the land red. Don't forget the islands!

Colour all of the water blue.

Canada

The Shape of Canada

Make the shape of Canada. Start at 1. Follow the numbers to 60.

Draw a big dot to show where you live in Canada.

Print the name of your town or city by the dot.

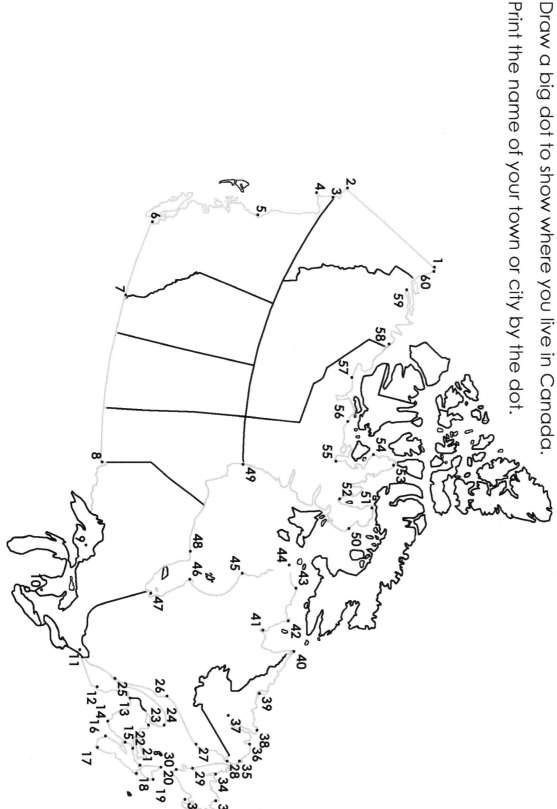

Show Me Canada!

Draw a big red circle around the map of Canada.

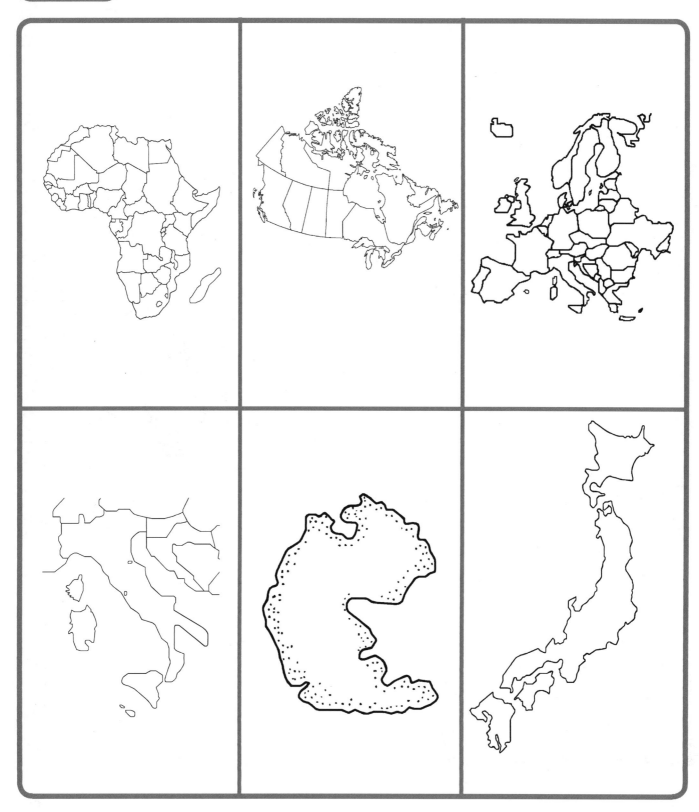

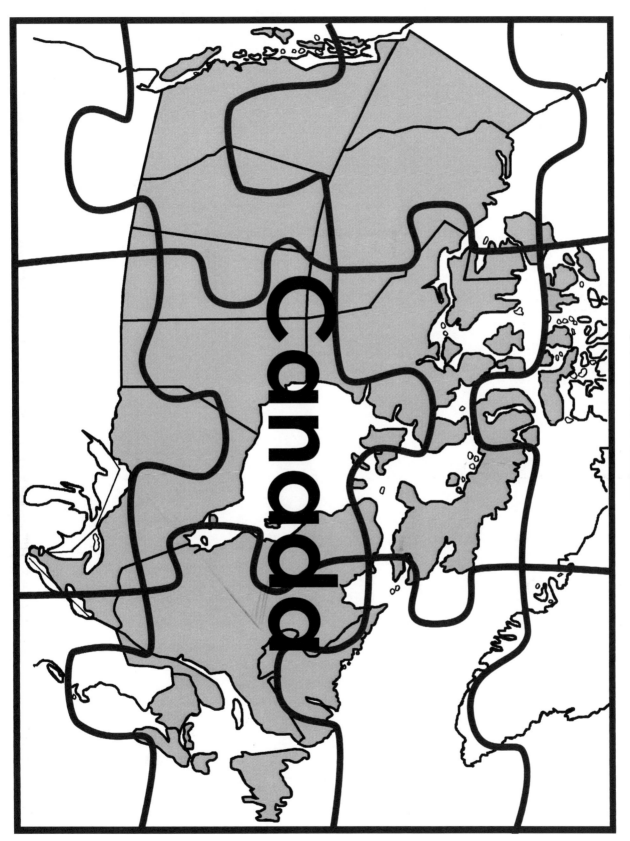

23

My Canada Puzzle

1. Use a ruler and a pencil to draw 6 straight lines on your map. These lines cannot cross each other.
2. The lines can go in any direction and they can touch each other.
3. With scissors, cut along each straight line to make a puzzle.
4. Scramble the pieces, then put the puzzle back together again!

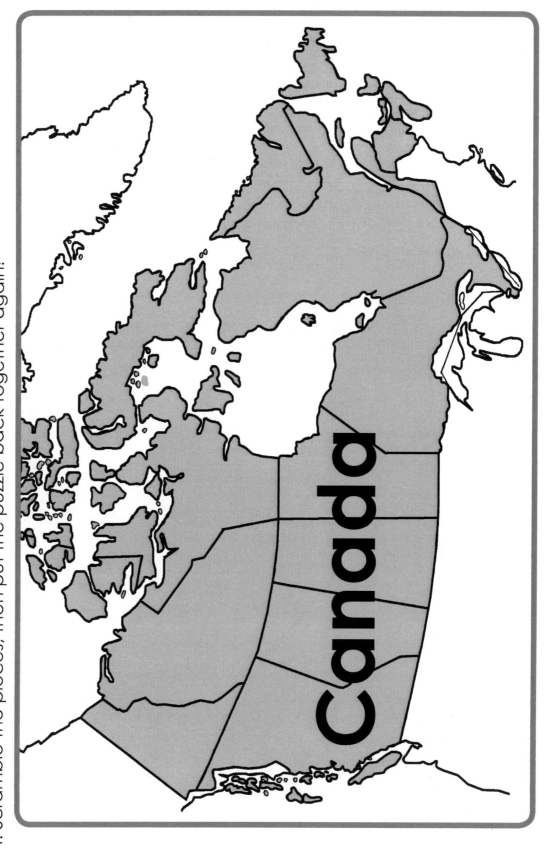

Canada from Space!

This picture of Canada was taken by a camera in a satellite high above Earth.

Draw a red line all the way around Canada.

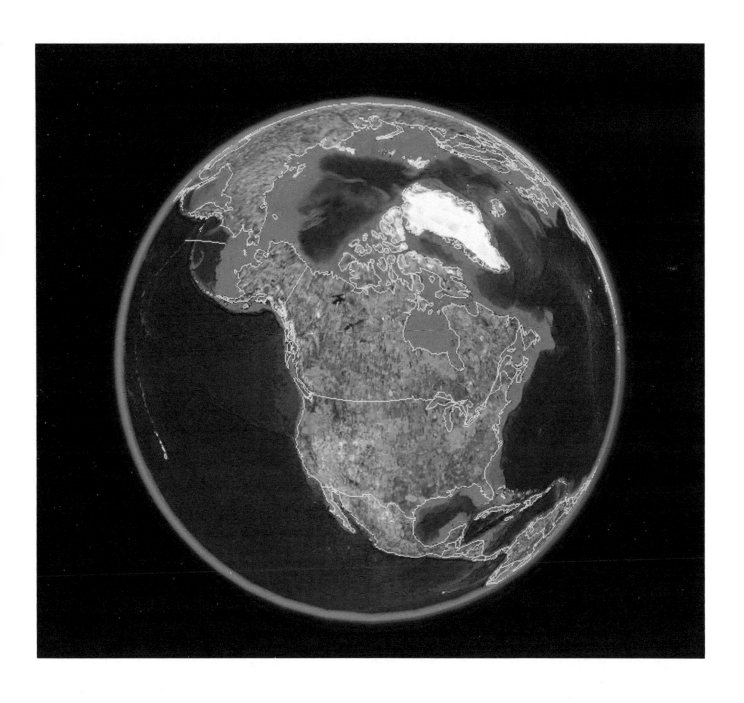

Explore Canada from Space!

Your teacher will help you to:
- ✓ Get on the Internet.
- ✓ Use a website with satellite images of Earth.
- ✓ Find satellite pictures of Canada.
- ✓ Zoom in and out.
- ✓ Search and explore.

Check off the places you saw:
- ❑ My province/territory
- ❑ The Great Lakes
- ❑ Vancouver Island
- ❑ Newfoundland and Labrador
- ❑ My town/city
- ❑ All of Canada
- ❑ Nunavut
- ❑ Hudson Bay

Add three more places you saw:
- ❑ _____
- ❑ _____
- ❑ _____

Canada from Space	A Map of Canada
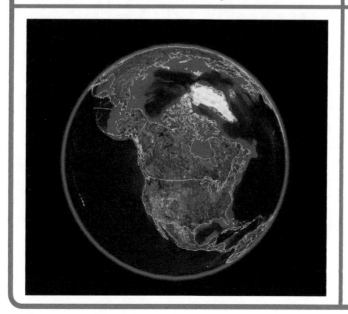	

A Globe

The Earth is our planet. When astronauts fly into space, they see that Earth is a huge ball. A much smaller model of the Earth is a globe.

Land and water are shown on the globe.

Land can be seen in many colours. Water is seen as blue.

Colour the land on the globe green.

Colour the water on the globe blue.

Put a big C on Canada.

CANADIAN MAPPING

Our Big Blue Planet

Our Earth from Space	A Globe
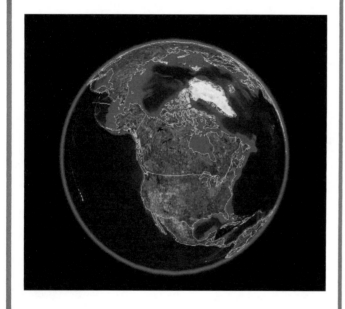	
From Space, our Earth looks like a big, blue ball. Colour the Earth light blue. Put a big C on Canada.	A globe is a model of the Earth. Colour the land light green. Colour the water light blue. Put a big C on Canada.

A Globe is a Sphere

A globe is a model of Earth. It is a sphere.
Half a sphere is a hemisphere.

Spheres | **Hemispheres**

Put an X on all of the spheres. | Put a ✓ on all of the hemispheres.

Globe Puzzle

Cut out the four puzzle pieces. Glue them onto another sheet of paper to create two globes. Put a big C on Canada.

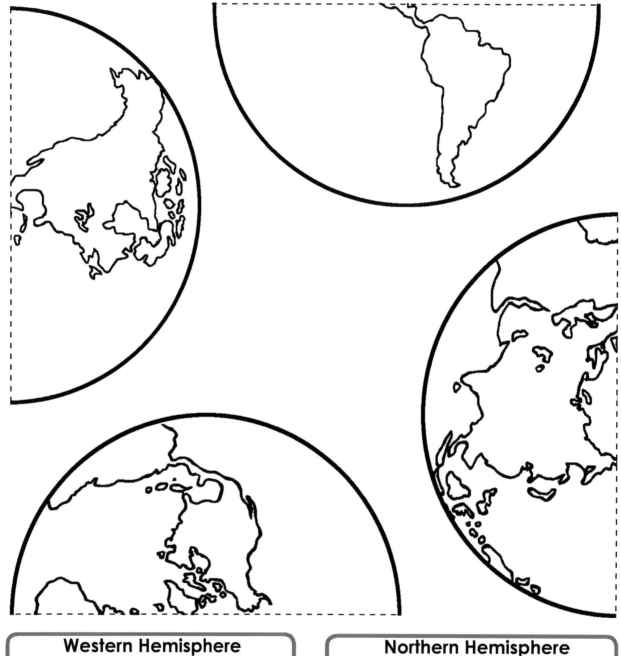

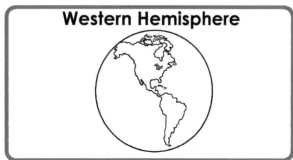

Western Hemisphere

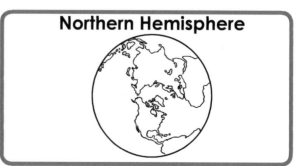

Northern Hemisphere

Where is Canada?

Print one of these words to complete each sentence.

East	West	North	South

Canada is _____ of the Equator.

Canada is near the _____ pole.

Colour the Equator red. It is very hot at the Equator.

Colour the North Pole and the South Pole blue. It is cold at the North Pole and the South Pole.

Print a big C on Canada.

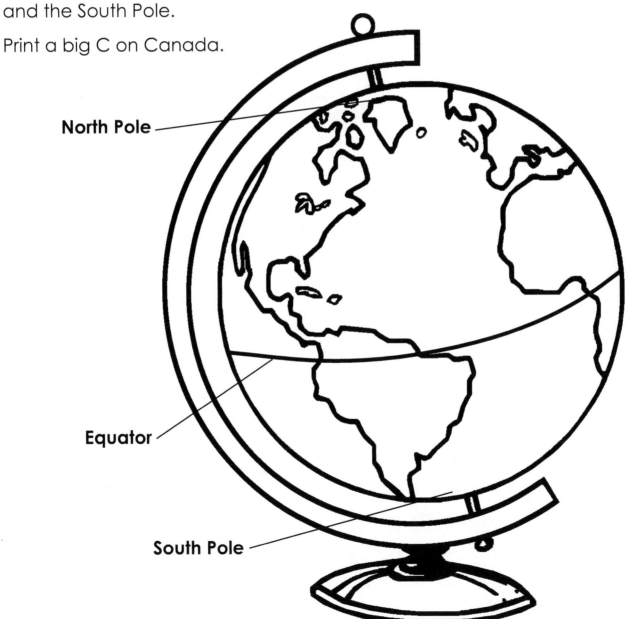

North Pole

Equator

South Pole

✦ CANADIAN MAPPING 🏳

Where in the World is Canada?

Cut the four labels below and glue them on the map of the world in the correct places.

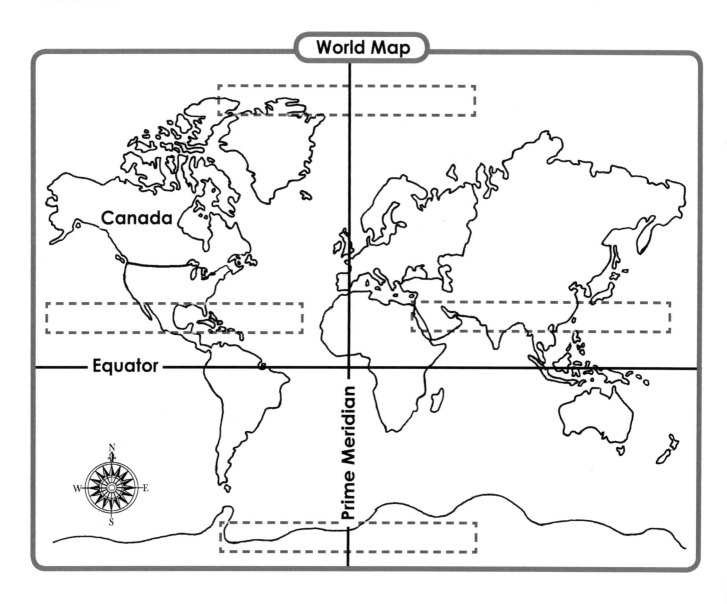

World Map

Canada

Equator

Prime Meridian

✂ --

| Western Hemisphere | Eastern Hemisphere |
| Northern Hemisphere | Southern Hemisphere |

★ CANADIAN MAPPING

Where in the World is It?

Draw a line from each ★ to one or more of these places on the map: North Pole, South Pole, Prime Meridian, Equator, Canada (The first one is done for you.)

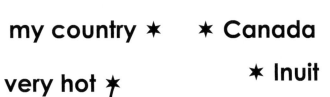

my country ★   ★ **Canada**

very hot ★

★ **Inuit**

very cold ★

★ **polar bears**

penguins ★

★ **lots of snow**

★ **lots of ice**

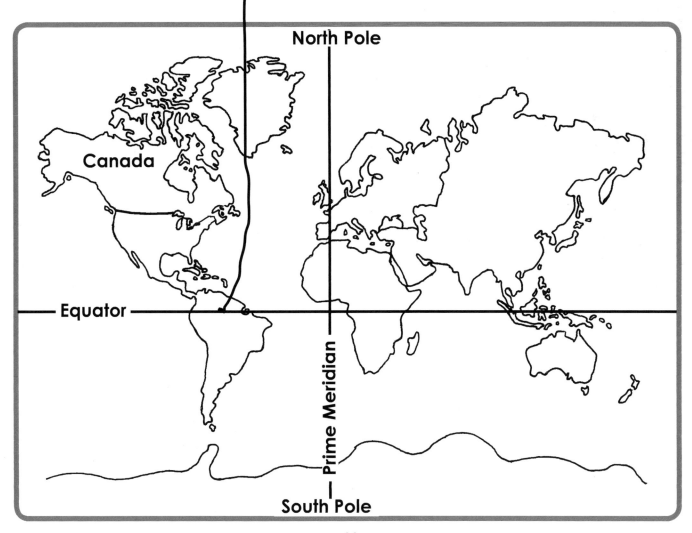

North Pole

Canada

Equator

Prime Meridian

South Pole

★ CANADIAN MAPPING 🇨🇦

Mapping Canada

Maps can be used for many purposes.
Cut the four labels below and paste under the correct maps.
Colour Canada red on each map.

Canada Physical

Aerial Photo

Satellite Image

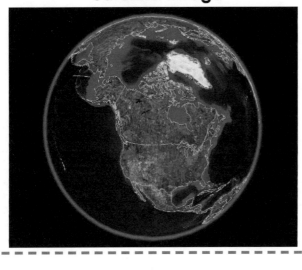

Canada Political

Used to see all of Canada's provinces and territories.	Used to see the way the roads are arranged.
Used to see what weather is coming to an area.	Used to see where the mountains are located.

More Mapping Canada

Maps can be used for many purposes.
Cut the four labels below and paste under the correct map.
Colour Canada red on each map.

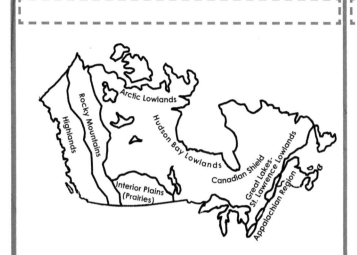

Use this map to see where very flat farmland is found.

Use this map when searching for something.

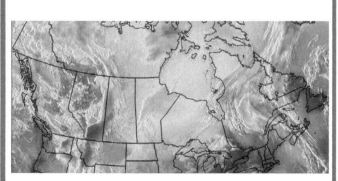

Use this map to see if the weather is good for flying an airplane.

Use this map to see the shapes of the provinces and territories.

✂

Satellite Image	Aerial Photo
Canada Political	Canada Physical

SSJ1-70 Canadian Mapping Big Book

Symbols of Canada

Symbols are pictures that represent a word or words.
Use scissors to cut out the symbols of Canada.
Paste them into the right column on the graphic organizer.

Maple Tree	People	Animals

◆ CANADIAN MAPPING

Neighbourhood Map-Legend and Symbols

In the Legend, draw a symbol beside each word.
Draw the symbols beside their numbers on the map.

Map

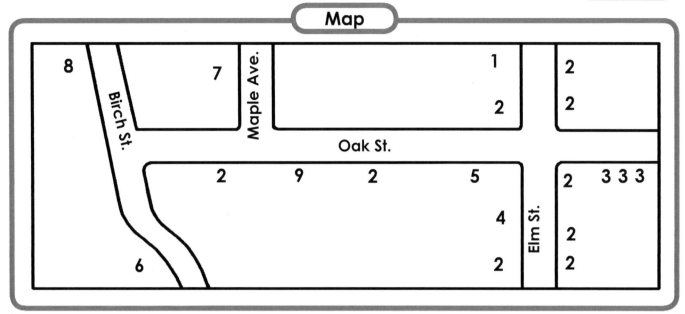

Legend

1	[ ]	school	4	[ ]	church	7	[ ]	library
2	[ ]	house	5	[ ]	hospital	8	[ ]	police station
3	[ ]	apartments	6	[ ]	flower shop	9	[ ]	post office

Name the Streets

Apartment Buildings _____

Houses _____

School _____

Church _____

Post Office _____

Library _____

Flower Shop _____

Map a Room! Using Symbols

This is a picture of a bedroom.

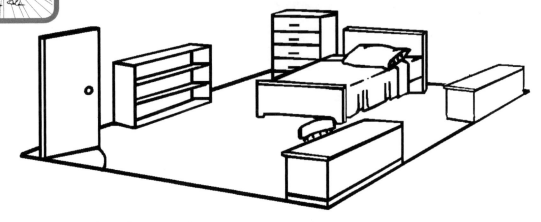

This is the same bedroom drawn as a map.

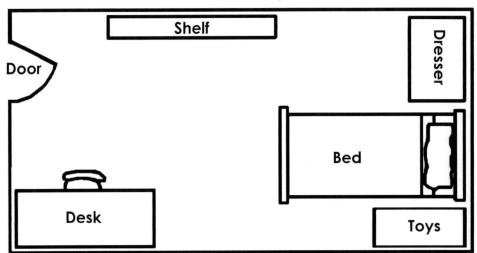

Choose a room in your school or in your house. Look at where each big piece of furniture is. Choose a different **symbol** for each thing and draw it like a map in the space below.

Mapping Our Kitchen – Making Symbols

Draw symbols for these things from your kitchen. Add other things you have in your kitchen.

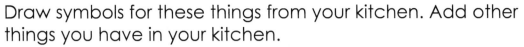

refrigerator (fridge)	table
stove	chairs
sink	dishwasher
counter	cupboards

Use your symbols to create a map of your kitchen.

A Map of My Kitchen

Pretend you are looking down at your kitchen from above. Draw a map of your kitchen using the symbols you have created. Make a Legend and add your symbols to it. Give your map a great title.

Legend

Finding Canadian Cities

Beside each of these Canadian cities draw the correct symbol.
* or O

___ Ottawa   ___ Vancouver   ___ Montreal

___ Charlottetown   ___ Toronto   ___ Churchill

___ Iqaluit   ___ Whitehorse   ___ Halifax

Use a map of Canada to complete the chart with the names of capital cities.

Province	Capital City
British Columbia	
Alberta	
Saskatchewan	
Manitoba	
Ontario	
Quebec	
New Brunswick	
Nova Scotia	
Prince Edward Island	
Newfoundland and Labrador	
Territory	**Capital City**
Yukon	
Northwest Territories	
Nunavut	

Colouring Canada

Arctic Ocean

Atlantic Ocean

Pacific Ocean

Newfoundland & Labrador

St. John's

Prince Edward Island

Charlottetown

Halifax

Nova Scotia

Fredericton

New Brunswick

Québec

Québec City

Montreal

Ottawa

Toronto

Ontario

Iqaluit

Nunavut

Churchill

Manitoba

Winnipeg

Saskatchewan

Regina

Yellowknife

Northwest Territories

Alberta

Edmonton

Calgary

Yukon

Whitehorse

British Columbia

Vancouver

Victoria

Legend
* capital city
o city

Colours on a Map

Colours on a map help us see the places very well.

Colour the most westerly province green.

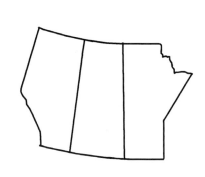

Colour the prairie provinces (plains) yellow.

Colour the most westerly territory red.

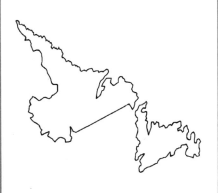

Colour the most easterly province grey.

Colour Canada's largest territory blue.

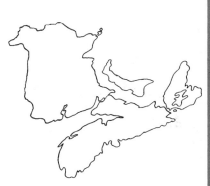

Colour the Maritime provinces pink.

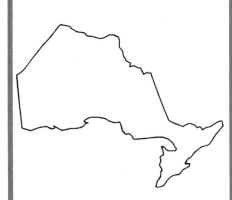

Colour the province with the Great Lakes purple.

Colour the largest province orange.

Colour the territory north of Alberta brown.

Compass Rose

A compass rose shows directions.
Print **North**, **South**, **East** and **West** on the compass rose below.

Print **N**, **S**, **E** and **W** on each compass rose.

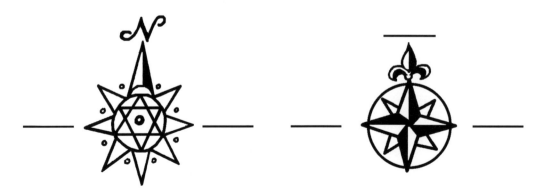

North, South, East, West

A compass rose tells directions on a map.

Circle **N** in North. Circle **E** in East. Circle **S** in South. Circle **W** in West.	Put **N**, **S**, **W**, and **E** on the compass rose.
North West East South	

Circle the compass rose on this map of Canada.

Mall Map
Krista is shopping at the mall. The mall map helps her find things.

Map of the Mall

_____ is North of Krista.

_____ is West of Krista.

Krista goes East. What can she buy? _____

Where is the clothing store? Circle one: **N S E W**

What Way?

Quentin's Family

What direction will they go?

 to see Space Rangers. _____

 to see Love in the Family. _____

 to see My Country. _____

 to see pretty flowers. _____

 to see The Story of Toys. _____

Aidan Loses Things!

When Aidan was on his Canadian holiday, he left things at places he visited. Cut out Aidan's things below and paste them in the right places. Draw a line to join Aidan's things and you will see his route.

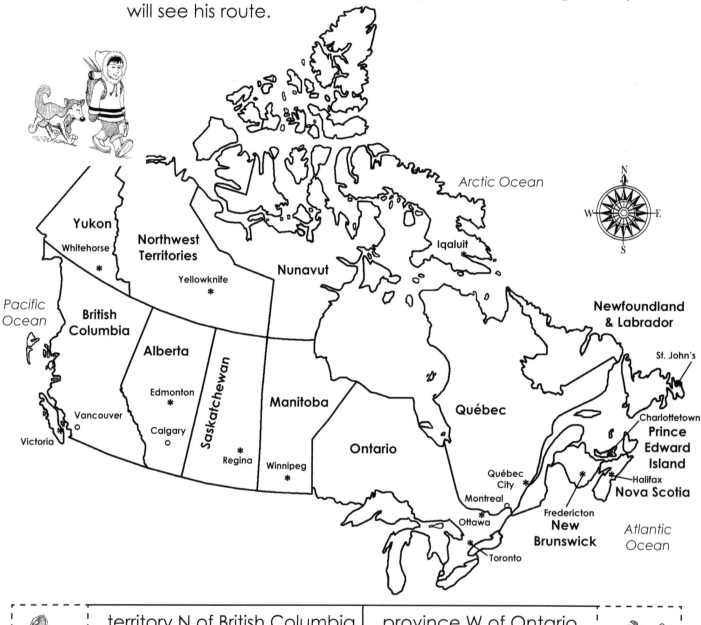

🔑	territory N of British Columbia – a key	province W of Ontario – a shoe	👟
🧥	territory N of Manitoba – a jacket	province E of Ontario – a cap	🧢
📓	province S of Northwest Territories – a book	province S of Newfoundland – a backpack	🎒

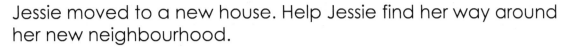 

CANADIAN MAPPING

Jessie's New House – Map Reading

Jessie moved to a new house. Help Jessie find her way around her new neighbourhood.

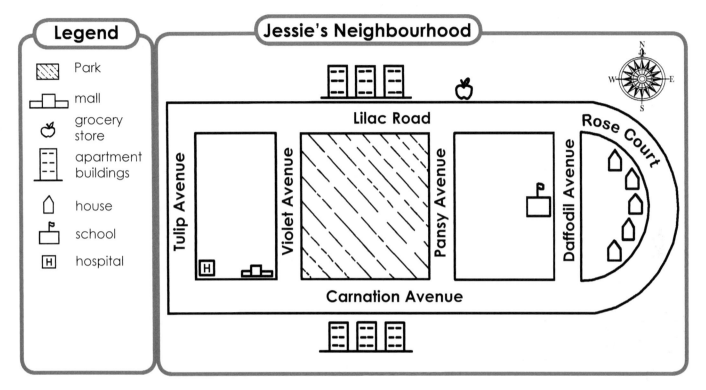

Print the street names for each:

the school _____

the mall _____

the hospital _____

the grocery store _____

Draw a swing set in the park. Add it to the legend.

The four streets around the park are:

_____   _____

_____   _____

What is West of the mall? _____

What is East of the school? _____

CANADIAN MAPPING

Using a Map Legend

Use this map of Canada to help answer the questions on the following page.
Use the Legend and the compass rose, too.

Legend

* * capital city
* ○ city

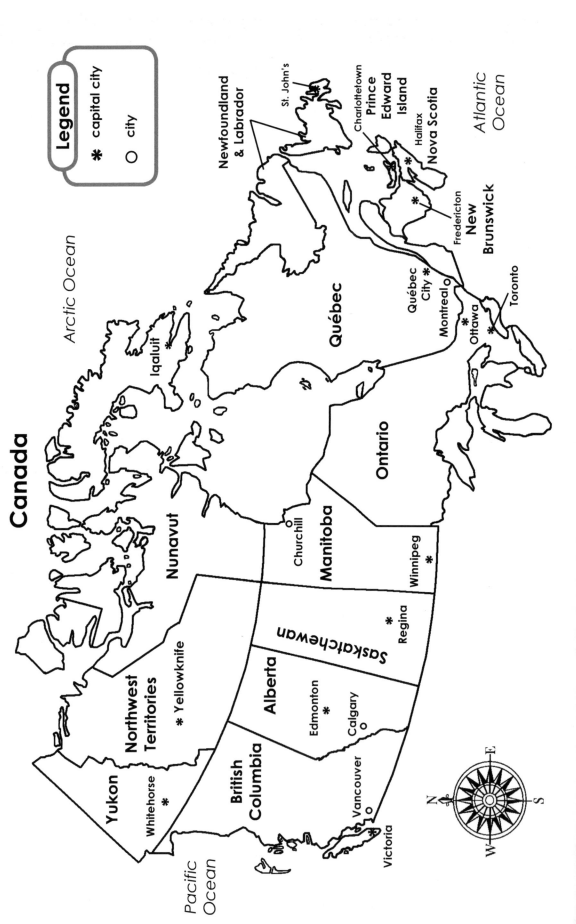

Canada

Arctic Ocean

Atlantic Ocean

Pacific Ocean

Newfoundland & Labrador

St. John's

Charlottetown Prince Edward Island

Halifax Nova Scotia *

Fredericton New Brunswick *

Québec

Québec City *

Montreal ○

Ottawa *

Toronto

Ontario

Nunavut

Manitoba

Churchill ○

Winnipeg *

Saskatchewan

Regina *

Northwest Territories

* Yellowknife

Alberta

Edmonton *

Calgary ○

Yukon

Whitehorse *

British Columbia

Vancouver ○

Victoria *

Iqaluit *

More Using a Map Legend

1. What is the capital city of Quebec? _____

2. What province is West of Alberta? _____

3. Charlottetown is the capital of _____

4. What city in Manitoba is north of Winnipeg?_____

5. What city is the capital of Nunavut? _____

6. Which ocean is east of Nova Scotia? _____

7. How many provinces are west of Saskatchewan?_____

8. What territory is North of British Columbia? _____

9. What city is South of Edmonton? _____

10. What ocean is North of Nunavut?_____

Complete the chart with words from the map of Canada.

Cities	Provinces	Territories

Be a Park Designer!

Make a map of an amazing play park. Use this model and checklist to help.

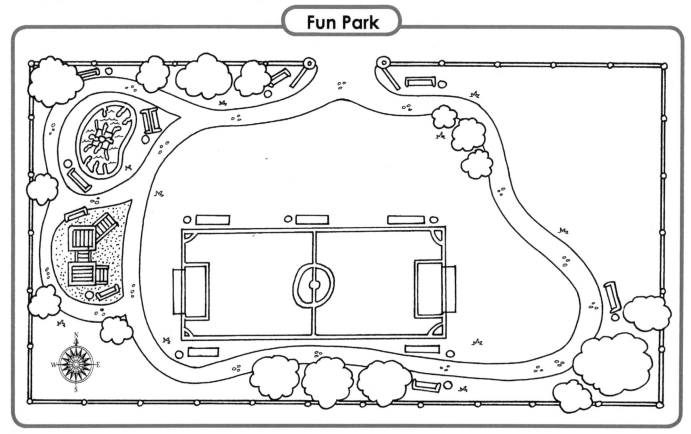

Fun Park

Fun Park Legend

gate | playing field | splash pad | climber | tree | bench | pathway

Map ✓ Checklist:

❑ Exciting title
❑ Symbols
❑ Legend
❑ Compass rose
❑ Trail or path

❑ Park gate
❑ Playing field S of gate
❑ Climber W of playing field
❑ Splash pad N of climber
❑ Add more symbols

Ideas: toboggan hill, skateboard ramp, skating rink, slide, etc.

CANADIAN MAPPING

My Park Map

Legend

Challenge!

Using directions **North**, **South**, **East** or **West** see if a partner can tell you what park place you are thinking about. E.g. "It is West of the skateboard ramp."

How Far Is It?

A map can tell distance when it has a scale.
Use a small paperclip to measure.

Scale

1

Circle the correct distance:

A to B	3	4	5	6
C to D	2	3	4	5
E to F	3	4	5	6
G to H	2	3	4	5
H to J	1	2	3	4
B to I	1	2	3	4

Using a Grid Map – Abigail's Toys

This grid map shows us where Abigail keeps her toys.

Abigail's Room

Print the grid location for Abby's toys:

1. doll _____A1_____
2. magic wand _____
3. markers _____
4. Canada flag _____
5. blocks _____
6. drum set _____
7. pail and shovel _____
8. car_____
9. radio _____
10. fire truck _____

Draw the following toys for these places on the grid:

D1 balloons   **A2** skipping rope   **C4** book   **B5** toy totem pole

Using a Grid on a Map of Canada

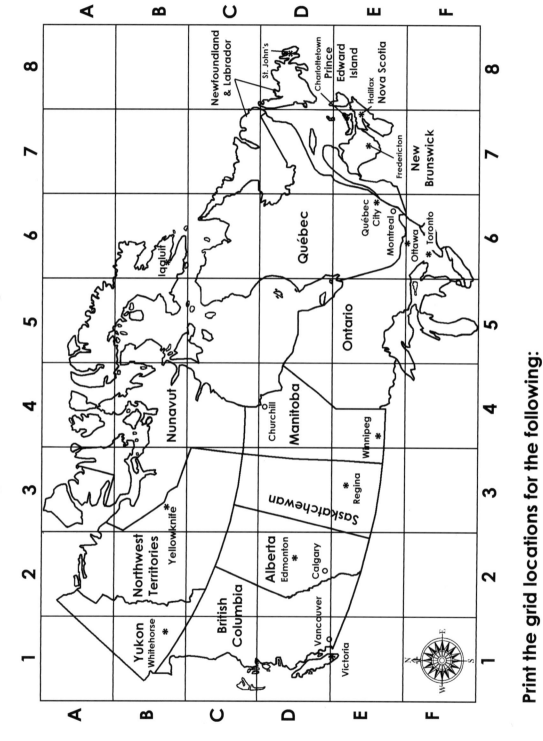

Print the grid locations for the following:

Yellowknife _____   St. John's _____   Edmonton _____

Quebec City _____   Victoria _____   Iqaluit _____

⬥ CANADIAN MAPPING 📖

What Are Those Lines?

Print these words on the correct spaces.

latitude	equator	North	South	degrees

1. The imaginary line at 0° latitude is the_____ .
2. The little circle after each measure is the symbol for _____.
3. N means _____.
4. S means _____ .
5. Parallel lines on a map are lines of _____.
6. Put a big red C on Canada.

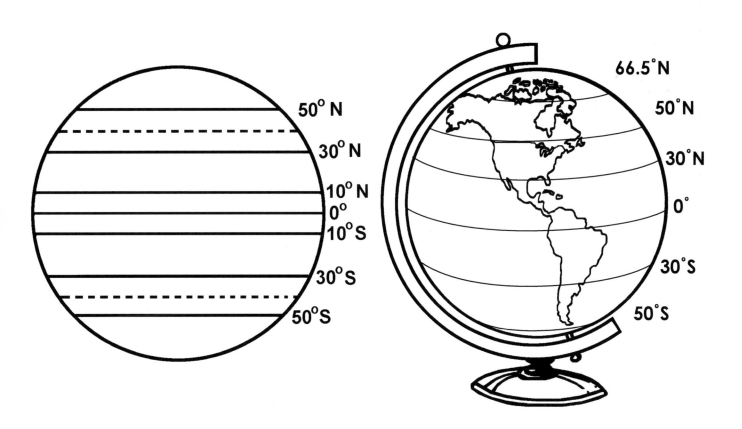

Parallels of Latitude

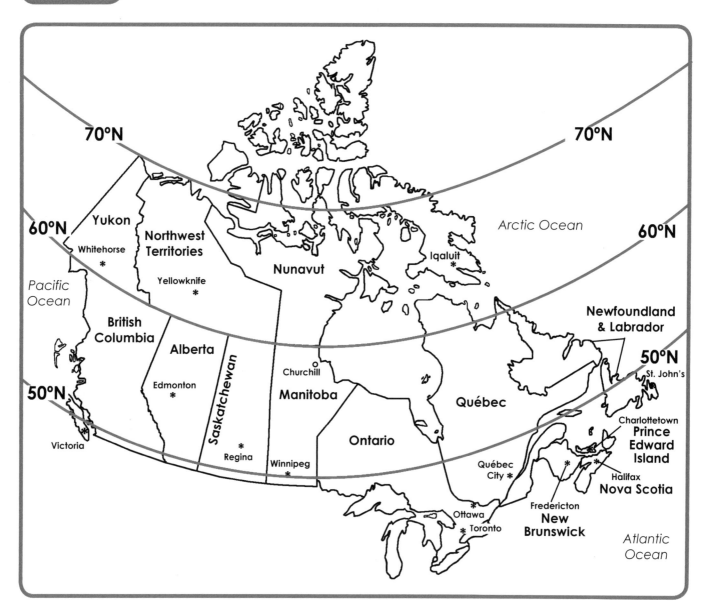

1. What city is at 50 ° latitude? _____.

2. Quebec City is closest to _____°.

3. Nunavut is between _____° and _____°.

4. What city is at 60° latitude? _____.

The Parallels and Longitude Game

This game is played like "Streets and Alleys." It works best in the gymnasium, a big empty room or outdoors.

1. Arrange the students standing in even rows and columns.

2. Choose a student not in the grid to be "It." Choose a student not in the grid to be the one who will chase "It."

3. The teacher will be the "caller."

4. When you yell "Parallels!" all in the grid turn to face the front with arms straight out at each side about shoulder height, with fingertips almost touching those of the next student. This creates parallel rows for the runners.

5. When you yell "Longitude" the students in the grid all turn to face the same side. They will again have their arms out at about shoulder height, with fingertips almost touching those of the next student. This creates long rows for the runners like lines of longitude.

6. When you yell "Go," the runner (It) enters the grid.

7. When you yell "Run," the chaser enters the grid and attempts to catch "It."

8. The students who are "It" or "the chaser" must never touch a student in the grid. If they do, they must change places with the person in the grid.

9. As the chase goes on, yell "Parallels" or "Longitude," making a challenging and changing course for the runners.

10. If the chaser touches "It," he/she must change places with someone in the grid. Occasionally change the "chaser."

11. After you have played the game a few times, a student may wish to be the "caller." You can add some fun by yelling a different command, such as "Outside," and the runners must stay outside the grid until the next command.

Note: The same game could be played with commands "North/South" and "East/West," with those in the grid turning in rows with arms out according to the command you have given.

Find the Equator and the Poles on a Globe

Teachers:

1. Use a real globe to introduce North Pole, South Pole, Arctic Circle, Antarctic Circle and Equator. Introduce term: lines of latitude

2. Compare the globe with images of Earth from space. Have students approximate on these images the locations for North Pole, South Pole, Arctic Circle, Antarctic Circle, and Equator.

3. Play the game "Point and Say." Give the students riddles such as "An ice cube will melt here right away." Students answer by saying aloud "Equator" and pointing to it on the globe or on the drawing of the globe.

4. Relate each of these lines of latitude to an area of the body (see diagram).

5. Play "Simon Says" using lines of latitude. E.g. Simon says "Touch the South Pole." Students bend and touch their toes.

6. Students: Use a real globe, the diagram of the globe and your body.

   Make the following connections:

   North Pole – top of head

   Arctic Circle – eyes

   Equator – waist

   Antarctic Circle – shins

   South Pole – toes

Stand and play "Simon Says" using the words from the globe. E.g. "Simon says: Touch the equator." Everyone should bend and touch their waists. Take turns being the leader of the game.

Now Play "Simon Says!"

Colour!

Red	North Pole	Hair
Blue	Arctic Circle	Eyes
Brown	Equator	Waist
Green	Antarctic Circle	Jeans
Purple	South Pole	Shoes

Many Many Maps

Colour Canada red on each map.

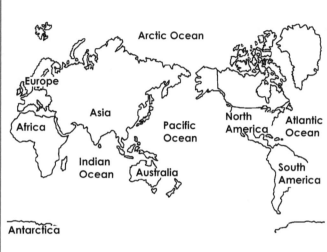

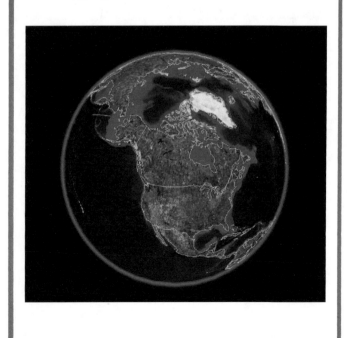

Global Views

Colour Canada red on each globe.

Put an X on the globe that does not show Canada.

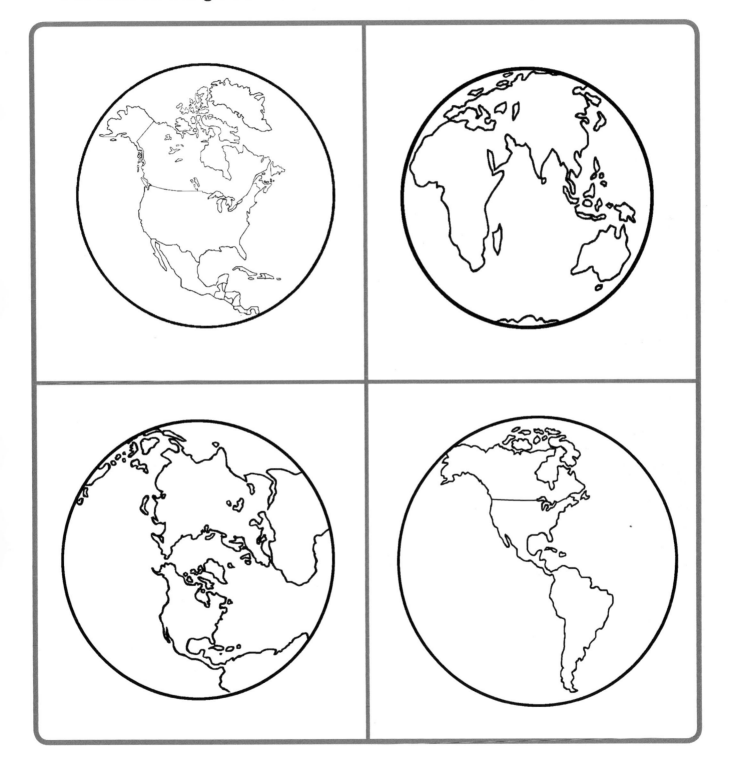

Canada Map Word Scramble!

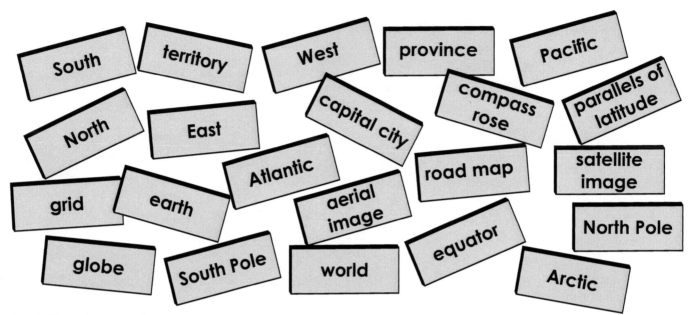

Sort the Canada Map Words. Print the words in the correct boxes.

MAP WORDS				
Directions	Oceans	Places	Lines	Kinds of Maps

Canada's Water

1. In this activity, students are introduced to names for major bodies of water in Canada.

2. Painted examples will be created for the following words: bay, strait, ocean, sea, basin, lake, river, harbour, and gulf. Others may surface during the activity.

3. Once the paint dries, it is necessary to demonstrate good labelling techniques: labels should all be horizontal, printing should be legible and consistent in size. When necessary (due to crowding), labels may include an arrow, and label rivers by printing the name of the river along its meandering line.

4. Equipment Needed:
   - Standard student desk-sized paper (one for each student)
   - A 250 ml sized pitcher of watery blue paint (Note: test the paint for fluidity ahead of time. It must flow, but not too quickly. It must be blue enough to demonstrate the water terms.)
   - Pencils for labelling.

5. Method:
   - The teacher will pore a very small "blob" of paint in one corner of each student's paper. Vary the location of this "blob" as you move from student to student. This will be either an ocean or a lake. (This is a good time to introduce the term source).
   - This step may require practice (using newsprint) before using better art paper.
   - Students will gently lift their papers and very gently tilt them this way, then that way. They should attempt to get their paint to flow out like a river with its tributaries.
   - While the paint dries, review the water terms using pictures, diagrams, and maps.
   - Students will label their diagrams with the water terms. This could be done by printing the labels or cut and paste. Not all terms will be displayed, but at least six should be on each paper. Note: you may wish to encourage creativity by asking students to make up names for their rivers and lakes.

Bay	Strait
Ocean	Sea
River	Lake
Gulf	Sound

★ CANADIAN MAPPING 🗺

Can You Find the Water Words?

Try to find these water words on the map of Canada. Circle these words on the map.

Bay	**Strait**	**River**	**Lake**
Ocean	**Sea**	**Gulf**	**Sound**

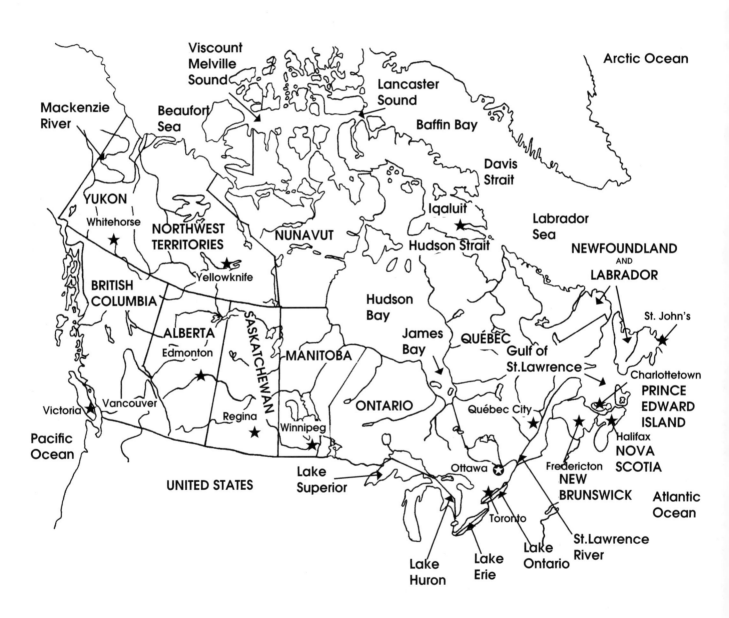

Trace around each province in green.
Trace around each territory in brown.
Colour your province or territory in red.
Put a big star ✱ at your town or city.

Canada is a _____.

Canada has ten _____.

Canada has three _____.

provinces	country	territories

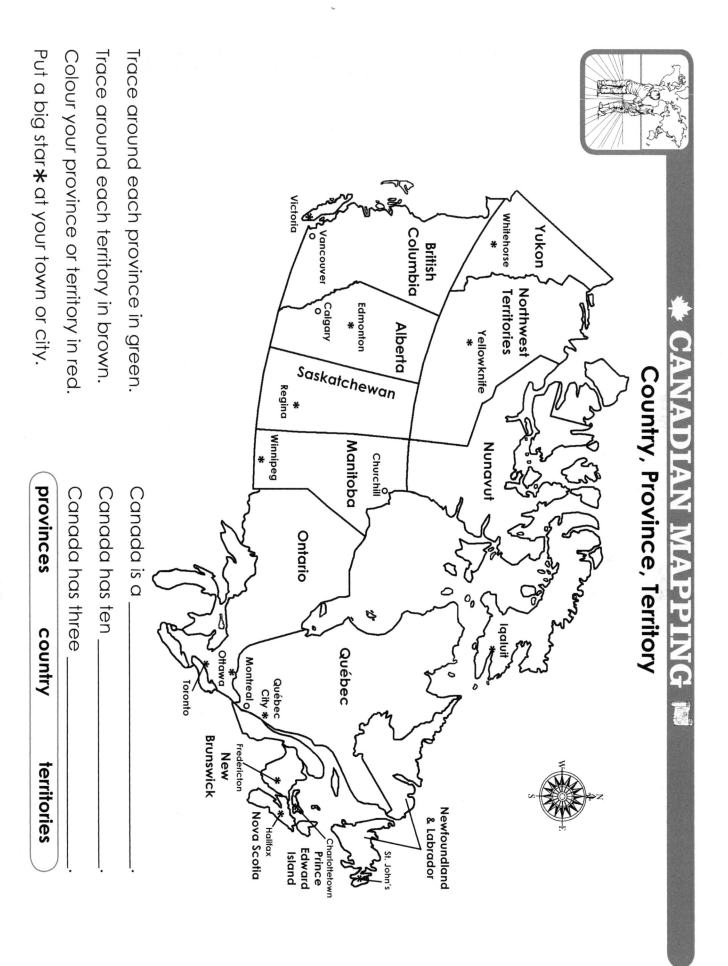

Victoria
British Columbia
Vancouver ○
Calgary ○
Edmonton ✱
Alberta
Regina ✱
Saskatchewan
Winnipeg ✱
Manitoba
Churchill ○
Whitehorse ✱
Yukon
Yellowknife ✱
Northwest Territories
Nunavut
Iqaluit
Ontario
Québec
Toronto
Ottawa ✱
Montreal ○
Québec City ✱
Fredericton ✱
New Brunswick
Halifax
Nova Scotia
Charlottetown ✱
Prince Edward Island
St. John's
Newfoundland & Labrador

W N E S (compass rose)

A Canadian Community Aerial View

Aerial View

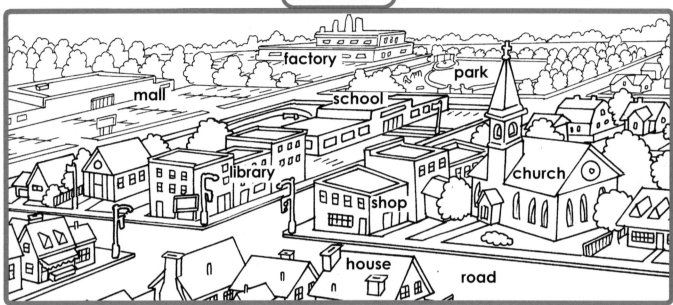

factory
park
mall
school
library
shop
church
house
road

Map View

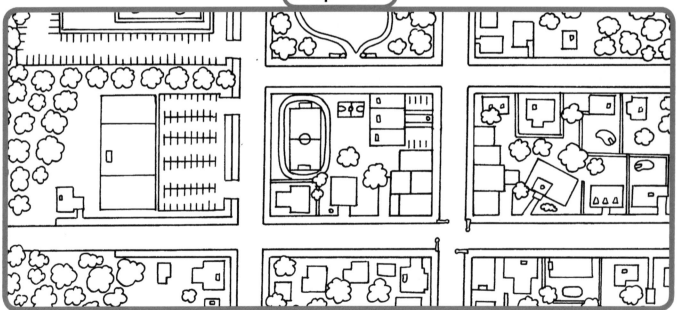

Label the "Map View" to match the "Aerial View."
Name three things that aren't usually shown on maps. (Hint: these are things that move).

1. _____ 2._____ 3._____

Where I Live

On the globe, draw a big star ★ to show where you live on Earth.

What is the name of your community? _____

Mark these statements right or wrong. Use a ✔ or **X**.

___ I live in a town.

___ I live in a city.

___ I live in a village.

___ I do not live in a town or a city.

___ I live in Eastern Canada.

___ I live in Western Canada.

___ I live in Central Canada.

___ I live North of the Equator.

___ I live in the southern hemisphere.

___ I live in the northern hemisphere.

___ I live in a province.

___ I live in a territory.

___ I live near the North Pole.

___ I live near the ocean.

Make a Road Map

1. On a big piece of paper on the floor, construct some houses and other buildings out of blocks.

2. Use a pencil to draw roads.

3. Make these buildings: ☑

   ☐ Town hall   ☐ Fire department

   ☐ Arena   ☐ Library

   ☐ Mall   ☐ Post office

   ☐ House   ☐ Farm houses and barns

4. Draw a compass rose in the corner. Label it with N, S, W and E.

5. Go over your pencil line roads with a marker.

6. Use a camera to take a picture of your map as you look down at it. Try to get all parts into your photo. Safely get as high above your map as you can. An adult will help you.

7. Use a marker to trace around the base of all of your buildings. Then take away all of the blocks.

8. Compare your map with your photograph.

Aerial photography: Taking photos from high above	**Bird's-eye view:** Looking straight down	**Map:** Uses symbols and drawings to tell how a place looks from high above
		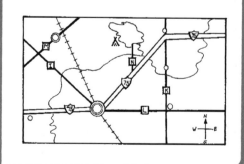

CANADIAN MAPPING

Lindsay and Anil's Canadian Community

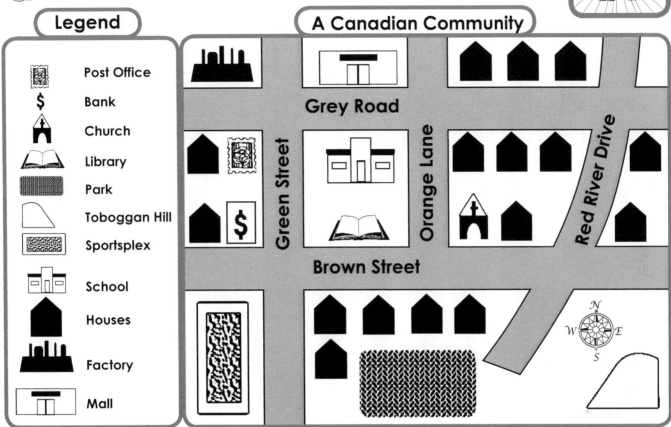

A community map can tell us many things. This map shows us the town where Lindsay and Anil live. Use the map to help you fill in the spaces:

1. Anil gets his favourite books here. _____

2. Lindsay plays hockey here. _____

3. Anil goes sledding here. _____

4. Lindsay and her mother buy socks here. _____

5. On the map, circle the place where they make cars.

6. Put a rectangle around the place to find a swing set and climber.

7. Anil lives in the house closest to the school. Colour his house purple.

8. Lindsay lives in the house closest to the church. Colour her house brown.

9. Use your pencil and draw the routes Lindsay and Anil would take from home to school.

A Walk in Our Schoolyard Checklist

Before the Walk:

- Clip your map to a hard surface such as a piece of cardboard or a clipboard.

- Make sure you have a pencil.

- Look closely at the map of your schoolyard. Trace your finger around the outside boundary of the yard.

- Put your finger on the door that you usually use.

On the Walk:

- With your teacher's permission, walk slowly around all parts of the schoolyard.

- When you see something from the checklist, check it off the list and place its alphabet letter in the correct place on the map.

- When you see something not on the list, make a quick sketch of it on the map.

Schoolyard Checklist

____A. Fence

____ B. Sand pit

____C. Baseball diamond

____D. Climber

____ E. Swing set

____ F. Bike rack

____G. Basketball court

____ H. Running track

✦ CANADIAN MAPPING 📜

A Map of Our Schoolyard

Use your checklist to help create a map of the schoolyard. Add other things you noticed in the yard. Challenge: put a compass rose on your map. (Your teacher will help you.)

Legend

Our Schoolyard

✹ CANADIAN MAPPING 1

A Walk in Our School Neighbourhood - Step 1

1. Think about the neighbourhood beside, behind and in front of your school.
2. Draw a picture/map of what you remember about this neighbourhood.
3. Put in as many details as you can.
4. Don't forget to show the school!
5. Challenge: add a compass rose to your drawing.
6. Reminder: Things on maps are usually things that do not move.

Our School Neighbourhood Checklist - Step 2

1. Compare your drawing with this list. Check off the things you put in your drawing of the school neighbourhood.

2. With your teacher, take a walk in the school neighbourhood. Check off the things you see. Add to the list anything else you think should be noted on a map.

Our School Neighbourhood	Things I Drew	Things I Saw on the Walk
• School		
• Streets		
• Church		
• Houses		
• Fire Hydrant		
• Trees		
• Fences		
• Apartment Building		
• Fire Hall		
• Store		
• Hospital		
• Mall		
• Shed		
• Barn		
• Gas Station		
• Car Wash		
• Hill		
• Schoolyard		
• Street Lights		
• Library		

CANADIAN MAPPING

Mapping Our School Neighbourhood-Step 3

1. Use your checklist. Your teacher will help you with the nearby streets.

2. Draw a map of the school neighbourhood showing the streets, things from the checklist and a compass rose.

3. When you are finished, compare this map with the first drawing of the neighbourhood.

♦ CANADIAN MAPPING 🏳

Assessment One – The Globe

(Students will need a pencil, a set of crayons and a sheet with large graphic depiction of the globe. Distribute one sheet to each student in your group. Read aloud each direction. Repeat as required, allowing the appropriate time for completion).

Name: _____   Date: _____

1. Trace the sphere blue. ☐

2. Put a big red C on Canada. ☐

3. Colour the land green. ☐

4. Trace the equator with a purple crayon. ☐

5. Is it hot or cold at the equator?
   Circle one: **cold**   **hot** ☐

6. Shade all of the northern hemisphere brown.
   (You will have to shade over other colours). ☐

7. Put a big N at the North Pole. ☐

8. Put a big S at the South Pole. ☐

9. Trace the Arctic Circle with a black crayon. ☐

10. Trace the Antarctic Circle with an orange crayon. ☐

For the teacher   Total _____

Assessment One – The Globe

Name:_____   Date:_____

Assessment Two – Canada in the World

(Students will need a pencil, a set of crayons and a sheet with a large map of the world. The map should have a compass rose and should show the major lines of latitude as mentioned below. Distribute one sheet to each student in your group. Read aloud each direction. Repeat as required, allowing the appropriate time for completion.)

Name: _____ Date: _____

1. Trace the equator with orange crayon. ☐

2. Trace around the shape of Canada with a red crayon. ☐

3. Draw three small boats in three places where there is water. ☐

4. Draw a big dot to show where you live in Canada. ☐

5. Put a big N at the North Pole. ☐

6. Put a big S at the South Pole. ☐

7. Trace the Arctic Circle with a black crayon. ☐

8. Trace the Antarctic Circle with a purple crayon. ☐

9. Is Canada in the **Northern** or **Southern** hemisphere? Circle one. ☐

10. Is Canada in the **Eastern** or **Western** hemisphere? Circle one. ☐

For the teacher   Total _____

Answer Key

A Globe is a Sphere: (Page 29)

Where is Canada?: (Page 31) Canada is North of the Equator. Canada is near the North Pole.

Where in the World is Canada? (Page 32)

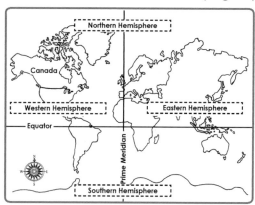

Mapping Canada: (Page 34) <u>Canada Physical</u>: Used to see where mountains are located. <u>Aerial Photo</u>: Used to see the way the roads are arranged <u>Satellite Image</u>: Used to see what weather is coming <u>Canada Political</u>: Used to see all of Canada's provinces and territories

More Mapping Canada: (Page 35) Canada Physical - shows very flat farmland; Aerial Photo – use when searching for something; Satellite Image – use to see if the weather is good; Canada Political – shows the provinces and territories

Symbols of Canada: (Page 36) Maple Tree: Canadian flag, penny coin, real maple leaf People: RCMP Animals: loon, moose, toonie coin, loonie coin, nickel coin, quarter, beaver and totem

Neighbourhood Map – Map Legend and Symbols: (Page 37)
Apartment Buildings: Oak Street; Houses: Oak Street; Elm Street; School: Elm Street; Church: Elm Street; Post office: Oak Street; Library: Maple Ave; Flower Shop: Birch Street

Finding Canadian Cities: (Page 41) Ottawa ✱, Vancouver O, Montreal O, Charlottetown ✱, Toronto ✱, Churchill O, Iqaluit ✱, Whitehorse ✱, Halifax ✱,

Capital Cities: British Columbia – Victoria; Alberta – Edmonton; Saskatchewan – Regina; Manitoba – Winnipeg; Ontario – Toronto; Quebec – Quebec City; New Brunswick – Fredericton; Nova Scotia – Halifax; Prince Edward Island – Charlottetown; Newfoundland and Labrador – St. John's; Yukon – Whitehorse; Northwest Territories – Yellowknife; Nunavut - Iqaluit

Mall Map: (Page 46)
Toy Store, Food Court, books, S

What Way?: (Page 47)
SW, E, W, S, NE

Jessie's New House: (Page 49)
Rose Court, Carnation Avenue, Carnation Avenue, Lilac Road, Four streets around park: Lilac Road, Pansy Avenue, Carnation Avenue, Violet Avenue. W of mall: hospital E of school: houses

More Using a Map Legend: (Page 51)
Whitehorse, Yellowknife, Iqaluit, Vancouver, Victoria, Edmonton, Calgary, Regina, Winnipeg, Ottawa, Toronto, Montreal, Quebec City, Fredericton, Halifax, Charlottetown, St. John's, Provinces: British Columbia, Alberta, Saskatchewan, Manitoba, Ontario, Quebec, New Brunswick, Nova Scotia, Prince Edward Island, Newfoundland and Labrador, Territories: Yukon, Northwest Territories, Nunavut

How Far Is It?: (Page 54)
A to B (4); E to F (4); G to H (3); B to I (1)

Using a Grid Map – Abigail's Toys: (Page 55)
1. doll A1   2. magic wand D2   3. markers A4   4. Canada flag B3 5. blocks C1   6. drum D4   7. pail and shovel C3 8. car B2 9. radio A3   10. truck C5

Using a Grid on a Map of Canada: (Page 56)
Yellowknife B3, St. John's D8, Edmonton D2, Quebec City E6, Victoria E1, Iqaluit B6

What Are Those Lines?: (Page 57)
1. The imaginary line at 0° latitude is the equator.
2. The little circle after each measure on the lines is the symbol for degrees. 3. N means North. 4. S means South. 5. Parallel lines on a map are lines of latitude.

Parallels of Latitude: (Page 58)
1. Winnipeg   2. 50° N   3. 60° N and 70° N   4. Whitehorse

Canada Map Word Scramble: (Page 64)
Directions - North, East, West, South, compass rose Oceans- Pacific, Arctic, Atlantic Places-capital city, province, territory, earth, North Pole, South Pole Lines-equator, grid, parallels of latitude Kinds of Maps-road map, satellite image, globe, world, aerial image

Country, Province, Territory: (Page 67)
1. country 2. provinces 3. territories

Lindsay and Anil's Canadian Community: (Page 71)
1. Library 2. Arena 3. Toboggan Hill 4. Mall

Helpful Teacher Notes for Specific Pages - Grade 3

It is well worth the time taken to insist early on that map colouring and labelling guidelines be followed. Explain that a map is intended to provide us with information. It must be legible. Record the following information on a chart and display it in the classroom to remind the children of the steps.

- Colour inside the lines using horizontal movements
- Colours should not mix
- Shade lightly
- Label in small, neat printing
- Label rivers by printing along the meandering direction of the river
- All maps should have great titles that immediately tell us how this map will be useful
- The best maps include a Legend or Key

Page 83 Canada in the World 1: Discuss the meaning of a political map and some of their many uses. Political map: map that emphasizes countries, states, provinces, territories, and cities

Page 84 Canada in the World 2: Pre-teach the meaning of continent. Show and name all of the continents using a large wall map. Focus on North America. Continent: largest landmasses on Earth; i.e. North America, South America, Europe, Asia, Africa, Australia, Africa, Antarctica

Page 86 Canada on a Globe 1: As your students observe, take some photos of your classroom globe from above and below. Provide time for students to look at these photos and discuss them.

Pages 88 and 89 Canada on Many Maps: if possible, show the students real examples of these maps, locating Canada on each. Be sure to point out to students that an artist has added white lines to the satellite image to help us see the shape of the land. (also if using page 25 and page 54) The two world maps provide an opportunity to talk about map orientation e.g. Atlantic – centered, Pacific - centered etc. Students in Grade 3 will require assistance with these pages.

Page 91 Pictures, Maps and Symbols: Teachers will find this page very useful to demonstrate the difference between a picture and a map. This is a good time to introduce the term "bird's-eye view."

**Page 92 Canadian Cities – Using Symbols
Pre-teaching idea:** Make a list of cities the students already know and have visited. Provide time for them to try to find these on maps. They will need help with reading the words on the maps. Some may wish to bring photos to school and tell about this visit to a city in Canada. Pre-teaching terms: City: an important or large municipality, usually having a larger population than a town, village or borough. Capital City: a city that is the official seat of government for that province, territory or Canada.

Page 93 and 94 Compare Two Provinces (Territories) – Using Symbols: These two pages will be excellent teaching tools. Discuss the items listed below the maps. After spaces are filled, take time to ask "How are these two provinces/territories alike? How are they different?" Create a large VENN diagram to summarize. Explain to your students the meaning and use for the small graphics of the Canada map on these pages: these will help them locate these provinces and territories. These pages will serve as a beginning for comparison. Students could use books, atlases and Internet sites to find further comparisons.

Page 97 Using a Map Legend – Map of Canada 2: Additional samples for use in pre-teaching:

- What city is NE of St. John's Newfoundland and Labrador? Iqaluit, Nunavut
- What city is SE of Yellowknife NWT? Winnipeg, Manitoba
- What province is W of Alberta? British Columbia
- What city is N of British Columbia? Whitehorse, Yukon
- What is the capital city of Ontario? Toronto, Ontario
- What city is further south, Toronto, Ontario or Ottawa, Ontario? Toronto, Ontario
- What province is East of British Columbia? Alberta
- Have students add orally to this list. Others in the group will answer.

♦ CANADIAN MAPPING 🏳

Page 101 and 102 Map of Ontario, Quebec and Labrador: Measuring Distance Using Scale: Discuss the need for a map scale. It is fun to show the students what happens if you try to draw a map of the classroom without having a scale. Needless to say the result is humorous and the map is not useful. Note: the students will require a great deal of assistance with these calculations. Answers will be approximate distances.

Page 105 Find the Equator and the Poles on a Globe: A teacher named Rebecca is credited with this idea on about.com Geography.

Equator: an imaginary line of latitude (0°) halfway between the North and South Poles.

Antarctic Circle: an imaginary line of latitude 66° 30' (66 degrees 30 minutes) south of the equator

Arctic Circle: an imaginary line of latitude 66° 30' north of the equator

North Pole: the point farthest north on the earth's surface. It is 90° north of the equator.

South Pole: the point farthest south on the earth's surface. It is 90° south of the equator.

More "Point and Say" clues:

- Penguins live here
- The "top of the world!"
- Hottest place on earth
- Polar bears like it here
- So cold skin will freeze (Two answers)
- A seal makes a tasty treat
- Watch you don't get a bad sunburn!
- Etc.

Pages 109 and 110 Canada on Many Maps 1 and 2: Students in Grade 3 will require assistance with these pages. They will require an introduction to the various types of maps shown.

Page 118 Canadian Mapping Game Ideas For the Teacher: Province/Territory Scramble: Additional "corner labels": Borders on USA, Atlantic Provinces, Closer to Pacific than Atlantic, Island provinces, etc.

Additional Ideas: Copy the map cards onto lightweight cardboard. Laminate them.

Two sets of the cards can be used in a game of "Concentration."

Pre-teaching will be required for recognition of provinces and territories: shape and location.

Canada map card sets can be useful for randomly determining a student's study topic for an inquiry (to select one province or territory). "Pick a card, any card."

Page 120 Landforms of Canada: Teaching idea – Provide pairs of students with a map of Canada mounted on cardboard. Challenge students to depict Canada's landforms (3D) using play dough. They will enjoy using popsicle sticks and toothpicks to create texture in the various regions.

Page 121 Are You Planning A Trip?

Copy this activity onto the chalkboard. Discuss.

Circle words that tell about Ontario's waterways:

travel	hydro-electricity	tobogganing
chocolate	fishing	shipping
hunting	sea life	vacations
drinking water	water for crops	books
computers	ice fishing	cottages

Page 129 Physical Map of Canada: Discuss the uses for a physical map. Go over the main regions of Canada as noted on the map. Make a list of these with small drawings beside each to help students remember what those areas are like. If possible, show photographs taken in each region.

CANADIAN MAPPING 🏴

Canada in the World-1

A **map** is a picture of a place. This is a **political** map. It shows the names of the continents. This map shows all of our world. We can use this map to see where Canada is in the world.

1. Colour all of the **water** blue.

2. Colour **Canada** red.

3. Colour all of the other land green.

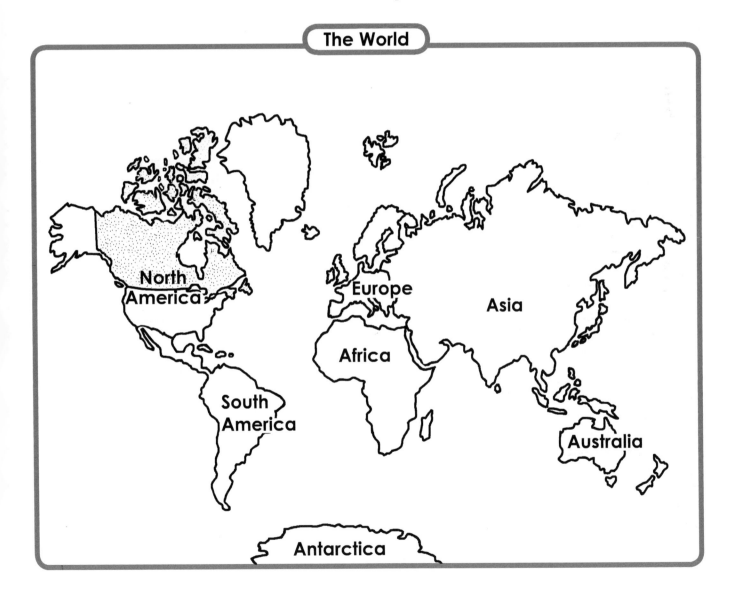

The World

North America

Europe

Asia

Africa

South America

Australia

Antarctica

★ CANADIAN MAPPING 📜

Canada in the World - 2

1. Print the names of the continents in the correct places on the lines.

North America, South America, Europe, Asia, Africa, Australia, Antarctica

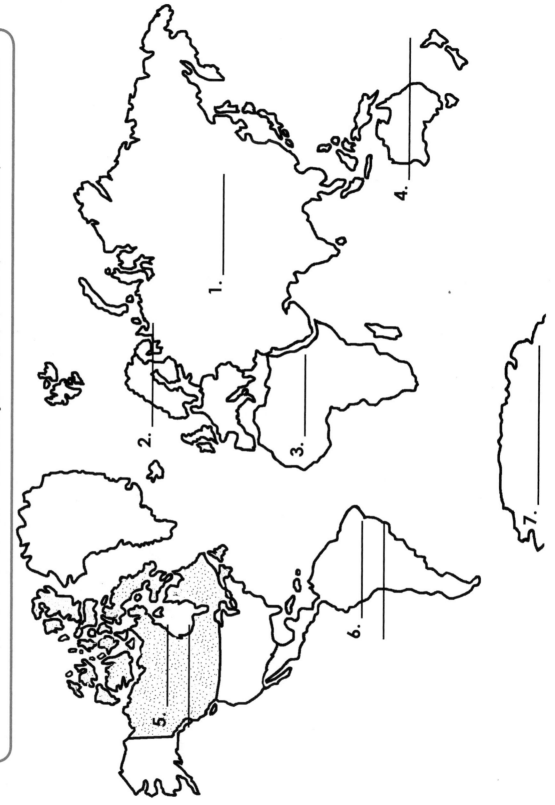

Canada in North America

Canada is part of the continent called North America. Canada is the largest country in North America. The other very large country in North America is the United States.

1. Colour all of the water on this map blue.

2. Colour **Canada** red.

3. Colour the other countries green.

4. Cut this label and paste it on the map.

Canada

North America

Canada

United States

Canada On A Globe - 1

⇦　Print a big red C on Canada.

Canada is in the **Northern Hemisphere.**　⇨
1.　With yellow crayon, **lightly** shade all of the Northern Hemisphere.

2.　Print a big red **C** on Canada.

Northern Hemisphere

Equator

Southern Hemisphere

Western Hemisphere

⇦　Canada is in the **Western Hemisphere**.
1.　With green crayon, **lightly** shade all of the Western Hemisphere.

2.　Print a big red **C** on Canada.

Eastern Hemisphere

Canada Sort

On the globes:

1. Colour Canada green. ☐

2. Colour the poles blue. ☐

3. Colour the Equator red. ☐

4. Colour the Prime Meridian black. ☐

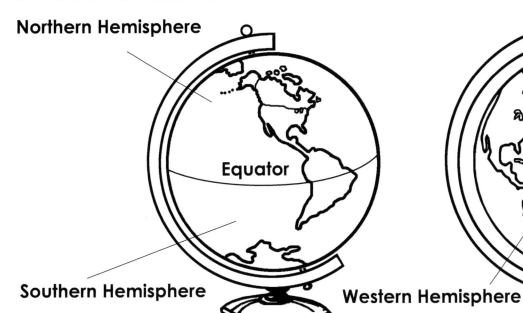

Northern Hemisphere

Eastern Hemisphere

Southern Hemisphere

Western Hemisphere

Equator

Prime Meridian

1. Sort these words. Print the words about Canada in the chart. Draw a line through all of the other words.

South of the Equator	North of the Equator	Far from North Pole
Northern Hemisphere	Western Hemisphere	Near North Pole

Canada

2. Beside each of these, print **HOT!** or **COLD!**

  1. Equator _____

  2. North Pole _____

  3. South Pole _____

Canada on Many Maps

Colour Canada red on each map.

World Map-1

World Map-2

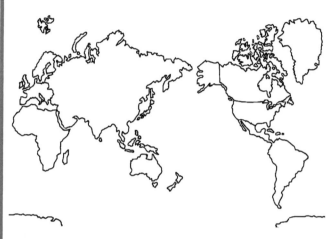

Satellite Image

North America

Canada On A Globe- 2

Colour Canada red on each globe.

Put an X on the globe that does not show Canada.

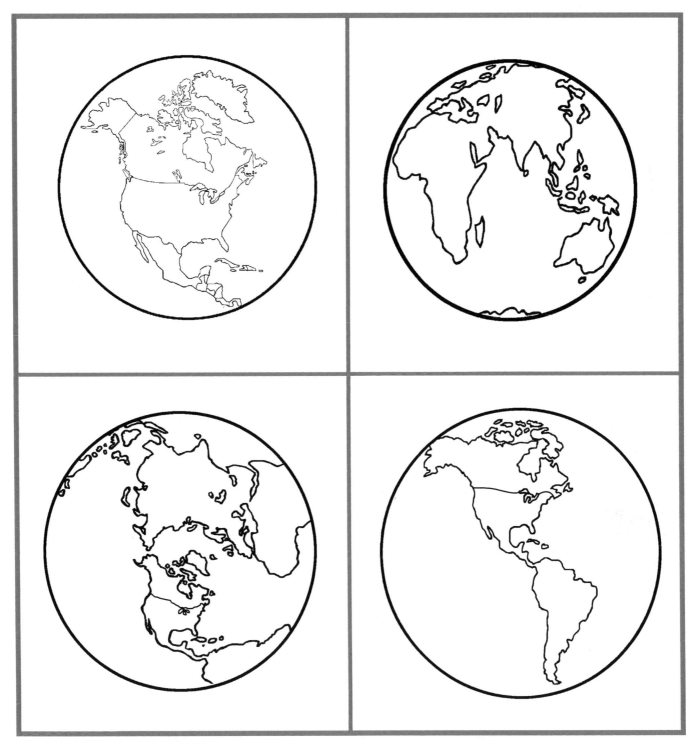

☀ CANADIAN MAPPING 🚩

The Continents

The continents are the seven large landmasses in our world. They are: North America, South America, Europe, Asia, Africa, Australia, and Antarctica.

Canada is part of North America.

1. Using a ruler, draw a straight line to join the name of each continent to its shape on the globe.

2. Try turning a real globe to find the seven continents.

3. With a red crayon, lightly shade Canada. Print a big C on Canada.

- **South America**

- **North America**

- **Asia**

- **Australia**

- **Antarctica**

- **Africa**

- **Europe**

CANADIAN MAPPING

Pictures, Maps and Symbols

This is a picture of a bedroom.

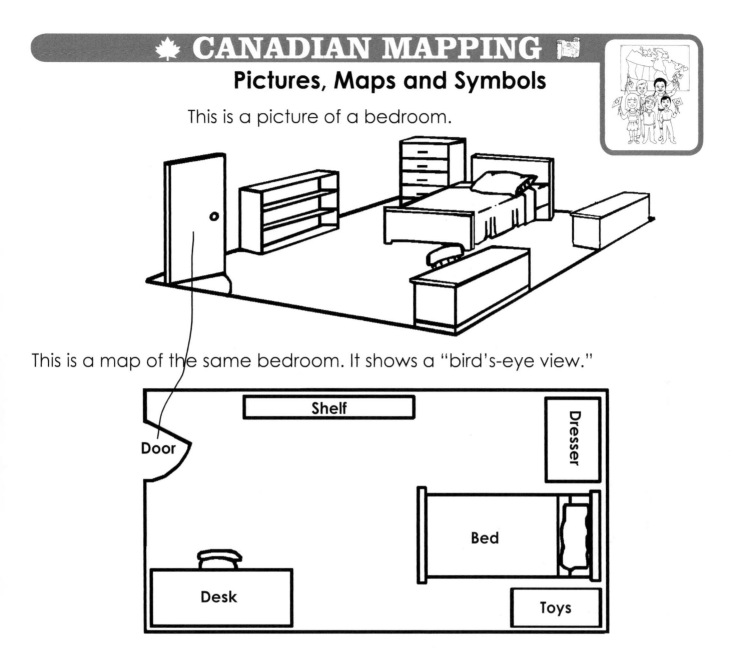

This is a map of the same bedroom. It shows a "bird's-eye view."

Draw lines from picture to map. The first one is done for you.

Draw the correct symbol beside each word in the Legend/Key.

Legend

1		Shelf	4		Door
2		Dresser	5		Desk
3		Bed	6		Toy Box

✦ CANADIAN MAPPING 🏴

Canadian Cities – Using Symbols

Use this map of Canada to find the locations for Canadian cities.

1. Circle the names of the capital cities red.

2. Circle the names of other cities blue.

3. Mark your city or town on the map of Canada with a black dot. ●

Legend

✳ capital city

○ city

— province

Compare Two Provinces – Using Symbols

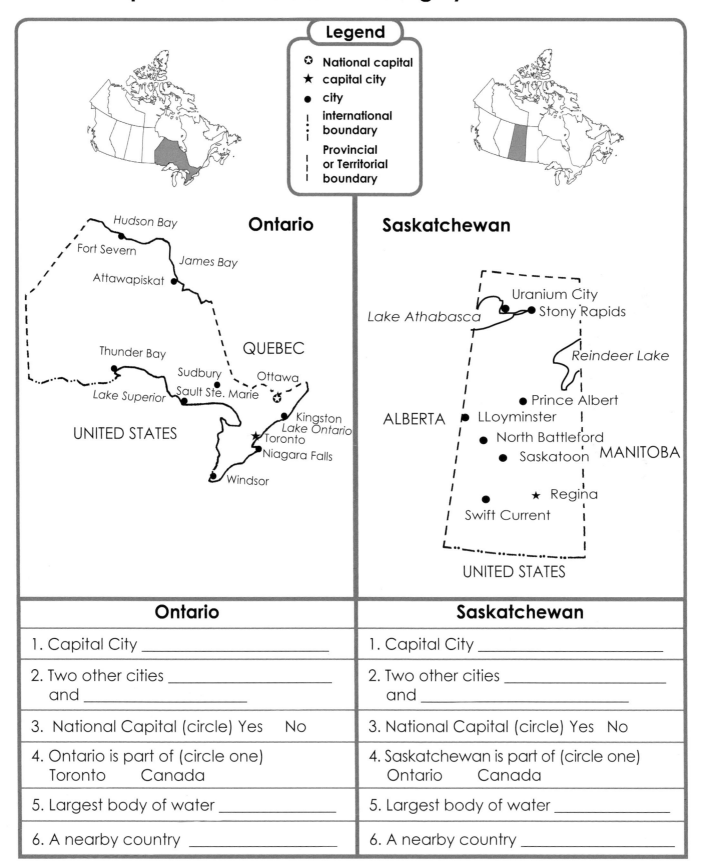

Legend
- ✪ National capital
- ★ capital city
- ● city
- ┊ international boundary
- ┃ Provincial or Territorial boundary

Ontario

Hudson Bay
Fort Severn
James Bay
Attawapiskat
QUEBEC
Thunder Bay
Sudbury
Ottawa
Sault Ste. Marie
Lake Superior
Kingston
Lake Ontario
UNITED STATES
Toronto
Niagara Falls
Windsor

Saskatchewan

Uranium City
Lake Athabasca
Stony Rapids
Reindeer Lake
Prince Albert
ALBERTA
LLoyminster
North Battleford
Saskatoon
MANITOBA
Regina
Swift Current
UNITED STATES

Ontario	Saskatchewan
1. Capital City _____	1. Capital City _____
2. Two other cities _____ and _____	2. Two other cities _____ and _____
3. National Capital (circle) Yes No	3. National Capital (circle) Yes No
4. Ontario is part of (circle one) Toronto Canada	4. Saskatchewan is part of (circle one) Ontario Canada
5. Largest body of water _____	5. Largest body of water _____
6. A nearby country _____	6. A nearby country _____

❋ CANADIAN MAPPING 📜

Compare Two Territories – Using Symbols

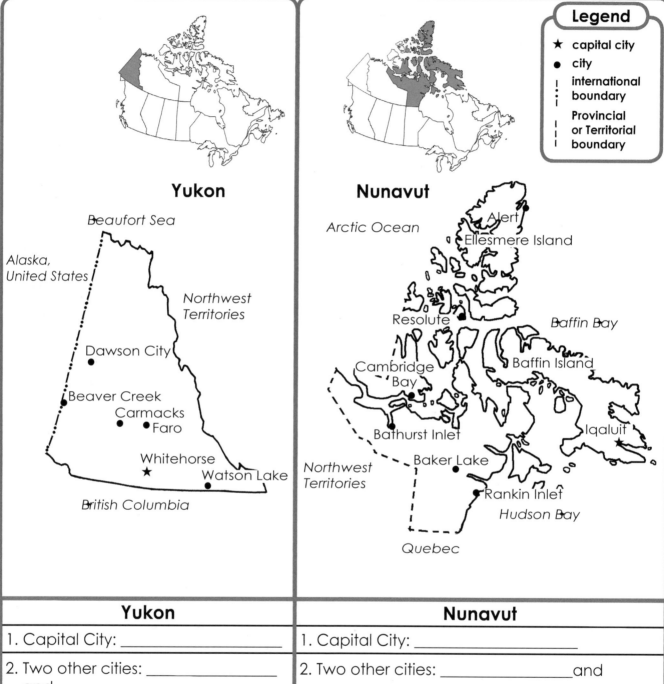

Legend
- ★ capital city
- ● city
- ⋮ international boundary
- | Provincial or Territorial boundary

Yukon	Nunavut
1. Capital City: _____	1. Capital City: _____
2. Two other cities: _____ and _____	2. Two other cities: _____ and _____
3. Many islands? (circle) Yes No	3. Many islands? (circle) Yes No
4. Yukon is part of (circle one) Canada Ontario	4. Nunavut is part of (circle one) Yukon Canada
5. Smallest territory? _____	5. Largest territory? _____
6. A nearby country: _____	6. A nearby country: _____

My Pencil's Journey – All Around Canada

1. Place the tip of your pencil on Northwest Territories.
2. Draw a line to the province SW (Southwest).
3. From there, draw a line going E (East) to the next province.
4. Next, draw a line that goes to a territory that is NE (Northeast) of here.
5. Draw a line to a province that is SE (Southeast).
6. Draw a line NE (Northeast) to a large island province.
7. Next, draw a line to the province that is SW (southwest).
8. Draw a long line going NW (Northwest) to the place your pencil began its trip.
9. List here the provinces and territories your pencil didn't visit on this trip.

Provinces that I didn't visit are:

_____

_____

_____

Territories that I didn't visit are:

_____

_____

_____

Challenge! Try this with a partner, using a different coloured pencil. Use directions that you create.

CANADIAN MAPPING

Using a Map Legend – Map of Canada -1

Use this map of Canada to answer the questions below.
The Legend/Key and the Compass Rose found on the map will help you with your answers.

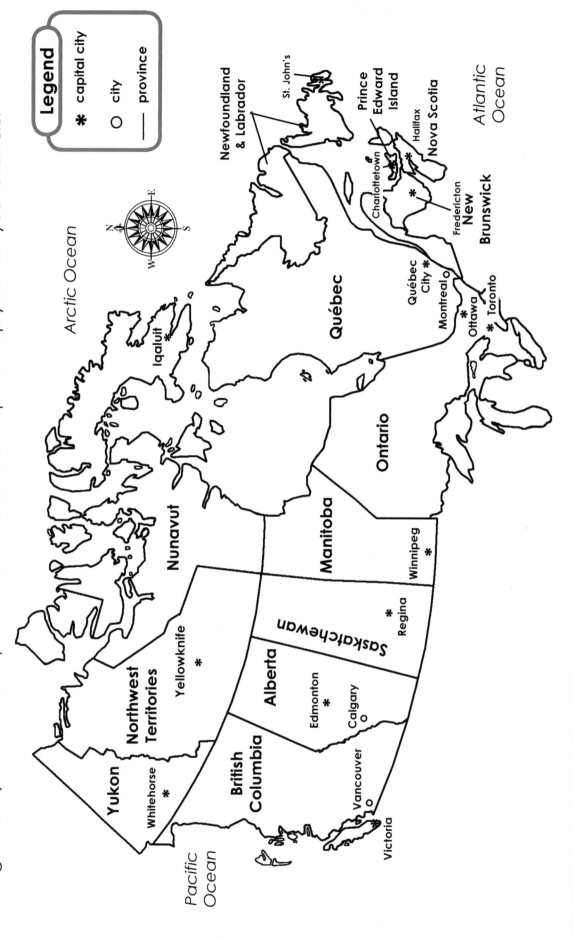

Legend

* capital city
O city
— province

Using a Map Legend – Map of Canada – 2

1. What is the capital city of Quebec? _____

2. What territory is NW of Manitoba? _____

3. What province is SW of Northwest Territories? _____

4. What province is SW of Newfoundland and Labrador? _____

5. Charlottetown is the capital city of _____

6. From Ontario, which direction do we travel to get to Alberta? _____

7. Which capital city is further North, Regina or Victoria? _____

8. What city in Manitoba is North of Winnipeg? _____

9. Which territory is Northwest of Quebec? _____

10. What city is the capital of Nunavut? _____

Complete this organizer with names of provinces and territories:

Provinces west of Ontario	_____ _____ _____ _____
Provinces east of Quebec	_____ _____ _____ _____
Provinces directly south of the territories	_____ _____ _____ _____
Provinces west of Saskatchewan	_____ _____

CANADIAN MAPPING

Be an Aquaplex Designer!

Everyone loves to go swimming at the aquaplex! A map will help them find their way around the building. Make a map of an amazing aquaplex. Use this model map and checklist to help.

Aquaplex

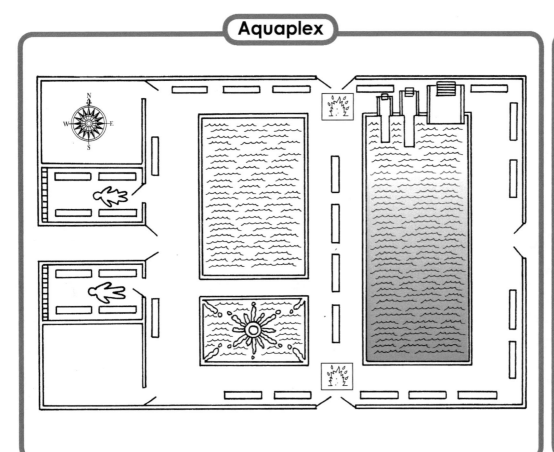

Legend

boys change room

girls change room

fire exit

shallow pool

splash pad

deep end

Map Checklist

- ❑ Exciting title
- ❑ Symbols
- ❑ Legend/Key
- ❑ Compass Rose
- ❑ Main doors
- ❑ Splash pad
- ❑ Other door

- ❑ Large pool with deep end
- ❑ Fire exit doors
- ❑ Large shallow pool
- ❑ Dressing room – girls
- ❑ Dressing room – boys
- ❑ Decide on ways to shade the hallways

Ideas: snack bar and tables, _____

_____

My Aquaplex Design

Pretend you are looking down at your aquaplex from above. Take a "bird's-eye view." Draw a map of your aquaplex using the symbols you have created. Make a Legend/Key and add your symbols to it. Give your map a great title.

Legend

Challenge! See if your map and Legend/Key work. Ask a partner to find things on your map. For example, you could say: "Show me the biggest swimming pool."

Map of Canada – Measuring Distance – Using Scale

With your teacher's help, draw a large star to show where you live in Canada. A bar scale helps measure distances on maps.
Read the bar scale on the map. Cut out the bar scale given below the map. Use it to measure the following distances.
Print the distances you measure in the chart below.

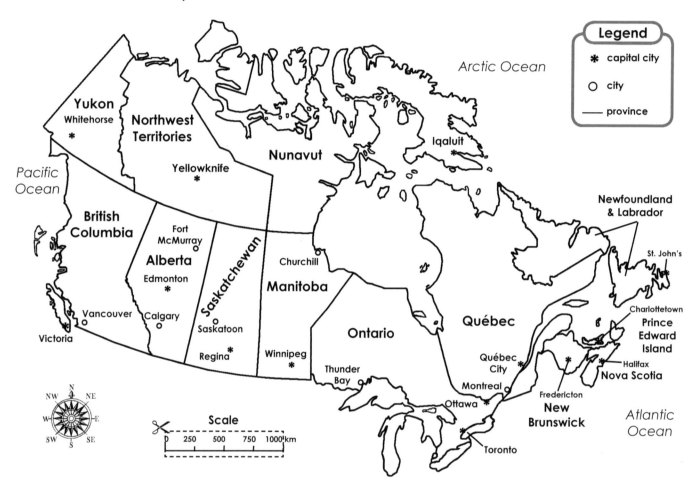

Where You Live	Place in Canada	Distance in km
	Iqaluit, Nunavut	
	Victoria, British Columbia	
	St. John's, Newfoundland and Labrador	
	Ottawa, Ontario	

Circle the greatest distance. Put a rectangle around the smallest distance.

Map of Ontario – Measuring Distance – Using Scale

A bar scale helps measure distances on maps. Read the bar scale on the map. Cut out the bar scale given below the map. Use it to measure the following distances. Print the distances you measure in the chart below.

From	To	Distance in km	
Hamilton	Moosonee		
London	Toronto		
Ottawa	Sault Ste. Marie		
Toronto	Windsor		
My Choice:			

In the column on the far right, do the following:

- Mark the shortest distance with the letter S

- Mark the longest distance with the letter L

Map of Quebec and Labrador – Measuring Distance – Using Scale

A bar scale helps measure distances on maps. Read the bar scale on the map. Cut out the bar scale given below the map. Use it to measure the following distances. Print the distances you measure in the chart below.

From	To	Distance in km	
Montreal, Quebec	St. John's, Newfoundland and Labrador		
Laval, Quebec	Havre- Saint-Pierre, Quebec		
Quebec, Quebec	Montreal, Quebec		
Val-d'Or, Quebec	Montreal, Quebec		
My Choice:			

In the column on the far right, do the following:

• Mark the shortest distance with the letter S

• Mark the longest distance with the letter L

CANADIAN MAPPING

Canada's Funland – Using Map Scale

Cameron and his family went to Canada's Funland. Use the map scale to help find out how far they walked on their visit. Use a ruler to measure the distances from place to place.

Map Scale 1cm = 5m

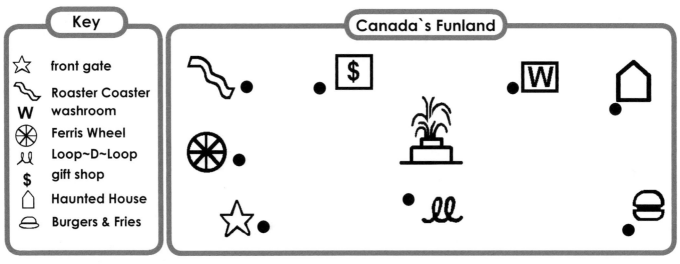

1. After paying at the front gate, they headed straight for the Ferris Wheel.
   They walked _____ metres.

2. After getting off the Ferris Wheel, Cameron wanted to ride the Roaster Coaster. They walked _____ metres.

3. When the Roaster Coaster was finished, they all wanted to visit the gift shop.
   They walked _____ metres.

4. After visiting the gift shop, they walked to the Loop-D-Loop.
   They walked _____ metres.

5. The family then visited the washroom. They walked _____ metres.

6. After the washroom, they all wanted to see the Haunted House.
   They walked _____ metres.

7. Cameron said that after the Haunted House, he would like a burger at Burger & Fries. They walked _____ metres.

8. When they were done eating at Burger & Fries, they went back out the front gate. They walked _____ metres.

9. The family walked a total of _____ metres at Canada's Funland.
   Hint: Use a calculator.

Parallels of Latitude

Parallels of latitude are imaginary lines on maps and globes. They run east and west around the earth parallel to the equator. These lines help us locate places on maps and globes.

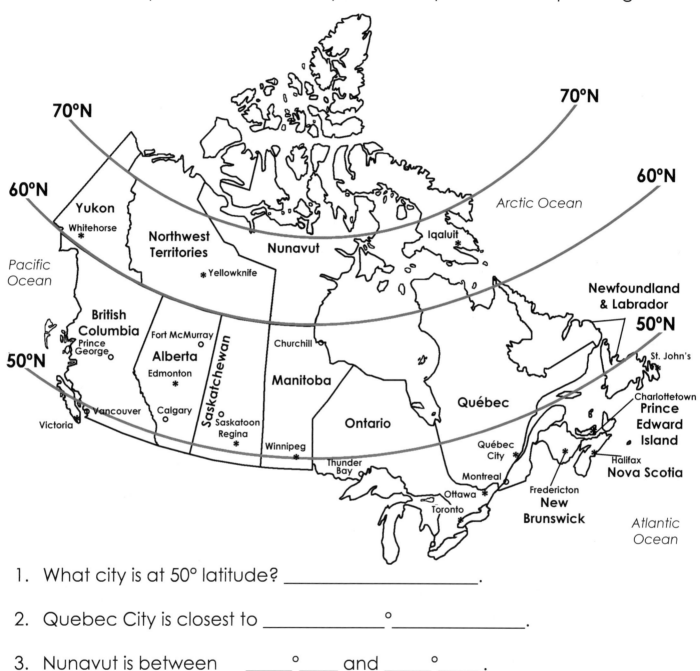

1. What city is at 50° latitude? _____.

2. Quebec City is closest to _____°_____.

3. Nunavut is between _____°____ and _____°____ .

4. What city is at 60° latitude? _____.

5. Find your community on a map or globe. What line of latitude is closest to your community? _____°____

Find the Equator and the Poles on a Globe

Teachers:

1. Use a real globe to introduce North Pole, South Pole, Arctic Circle, Antarctic Circle, and Equator. Introduce term: lines of latitude

2. Compare the globe with images of Earth from space. Have students approximate on these images the locations for North Pole, South Pole, Arctic Circle, Antarctic Circle, and Equator.

3. Play the game "Point and Say." Give the students riddles such as "An ice cube will melt here right away." Students answer by saying aloud "Equator" and pointing to it on the globe or on the drawing of the globe.

4. Relate each of these lines of latitude to an area of the body (see diagram on next page).

5. Play "Simon Says" using lines of latitude. E.g., Simon says "Touch the South Pole." Students bend and touch their toes.

Students:

1. Use a real globe, the diagram of the globe and your body.

   Make the following connections:

   North Pole – top of head

   Arctic Circle – eyes

   Equator – waist

   Antarctic Circle – shins

   South Pole – toes

2. Stand and play "Simon Says" using the words from the globe. E.g., "Simon says: Touch the equator." Everyone should bend and touch their waists.

3. Take turns being the leader of the game.

CANADIAN MAPPING

Globe Exercises

Colour!

Red	North Pole	Hair
Blue	Arctic Circle	Eyes
Brown	Equator	Waist
Green	Antarctic Circle	Jeans
Purple	South Pole	Shoes

Now play "Simon Says!"

Up and Down! – Introducing Longitude

Cartographers (map makers) sometimes add lines to a map to help us to find places more easily. These lines are imaginary because they are not really on the Earth. Some of these lines run north and south and they are called **longitude** lines or **meridians**. The longitude line that is zero degrees (0°) is called the **prime meridian**. The prime meridian runs through Greenwich, England. The other longitude lines measure the distance east or west of the prime meridian. The lines meet at the North Pole and the South Pole.

Lines of Longitude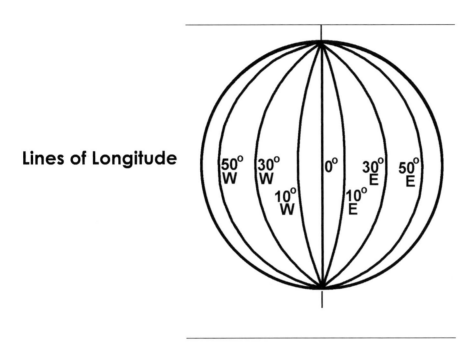

1. What is the line at 0° longitude called? _____

2. Which direction are the lines to the left of the prime meridian? Colour these red. _____

3. Which direction are the lines to the right of the prime meridian? Colour these blue. _____

4. Colour the prime meridian green.

5. The meridians meet at the top of the globe. Label this place "NORTH POLE."

6. The meridians also meet at the bottom of the globe. Label this place "SOUTH POLE."

Using Meridians of Longitude on a Map of Canada

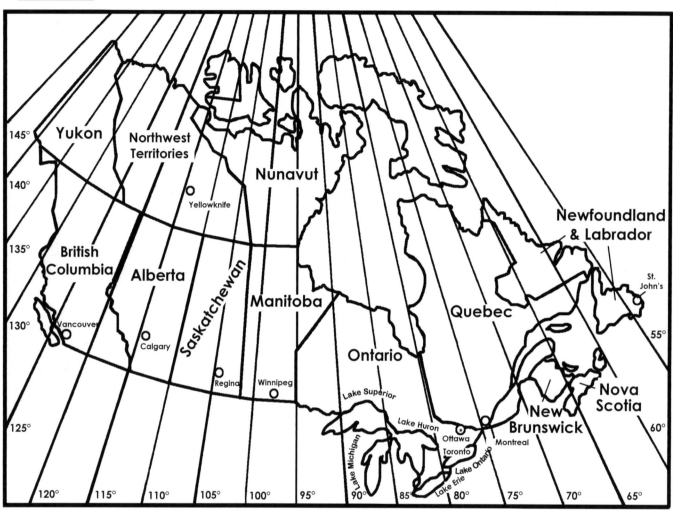

Use the map above to answer these questions.

1. What city is close to the 125° meridian? _____

2. What city is between 95° and 100° meridian? _____

3. The meridian at 75° lies between which two cities?
   _____ and _____

4. Calgary and Yellowknife are closest to which meridian? _____

5. Which city is east of the 55° meridian? _____

6. Regina is found near the _____ meridian.

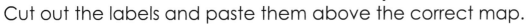
CANADIAN MAPPING

Canada on Many Maps - 1
Kinds of Maps
Cut out the labels and paste them above the correct map.

✂ -

| World Map | Globe |
| Road Map | Aerial Photograph |

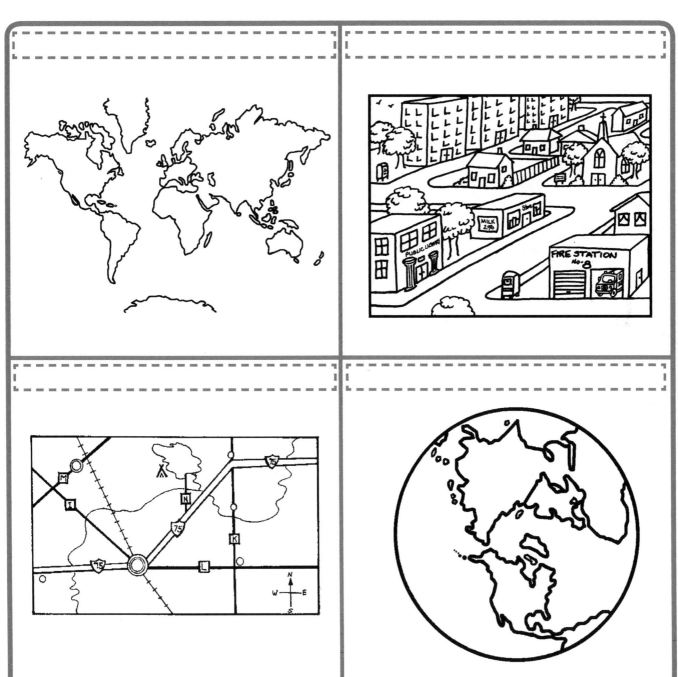

109

SSJ1-70 Canadian Mapping Big Book

Canada on Many Maps - 2

Kinds of Maps

Cut the labels and paste them above the correct map.

✂ --

| Physical Map of Canada | Political Map of Canada |
| Satellite Image | Map of North America |

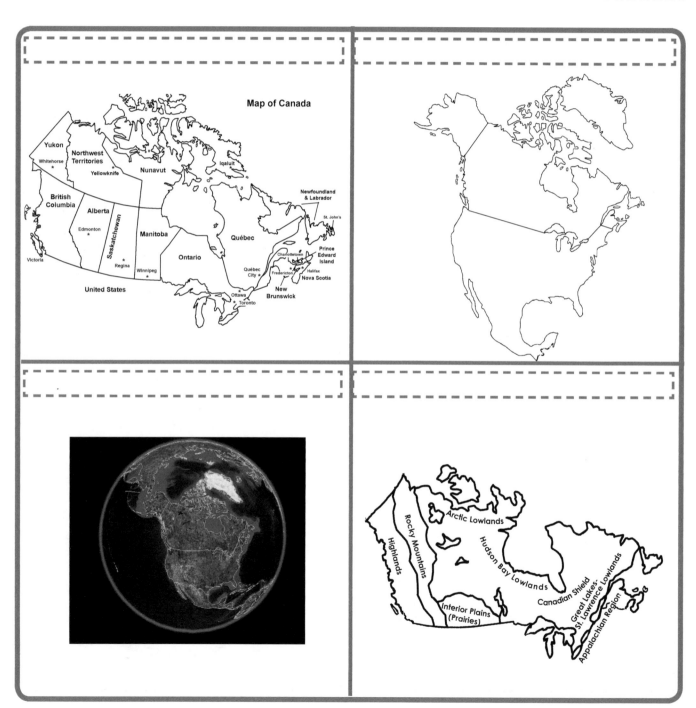

⬥ CANADIAN MAPPING 🏴

Mapping Canada

Maps can be used for many purposes. Cut out the four labels below and paste them under the correct map.
Colour Canada red on three maps.

Used to see all of Canada's provinces and territories.	Used to see the way the roads are arranged.
Used to see what weather is coming to an area.	Used to see where the mountains are located.

Canada Physical

Aerial Photo

Satellite Image

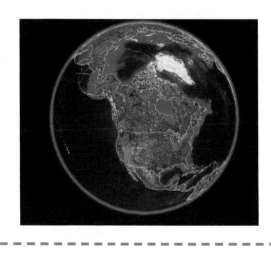

Canada Political

CANADIAN MAPPING

More Mapping Canada

Maps can be used for many purposes.
Cut the four labels below and paste above the correct map.
Colour Canada red on three maps.

✂

| Satellite Image | Road Map |
| Canada Political | Canada Physical |

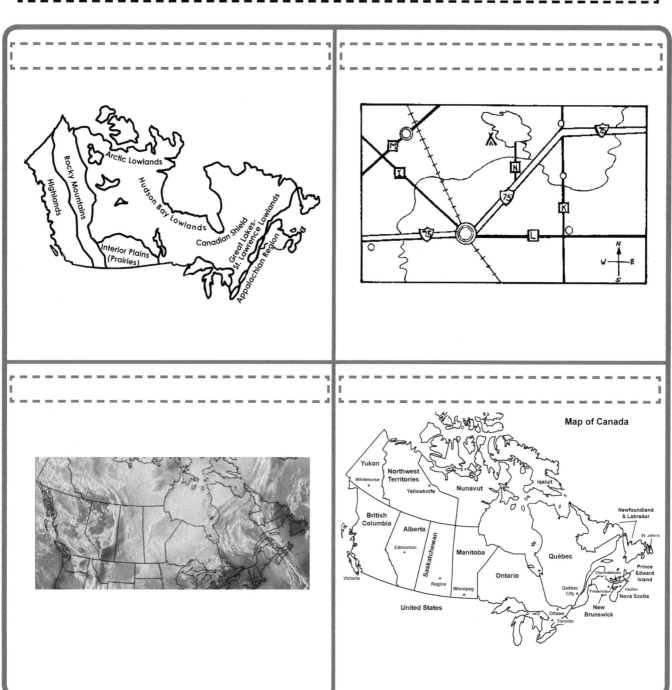

Canada's Provinces and Territories

Cut the labels and paste in the correct places.

Yukon

Northwest Territories

Nunavut

British Columbia

Alberta

Saskatchewan

Manitoba

Ontario

Quebec

New Brunswick

Nova Scotia

Prince Edward Island

Newfoundland and Labrador

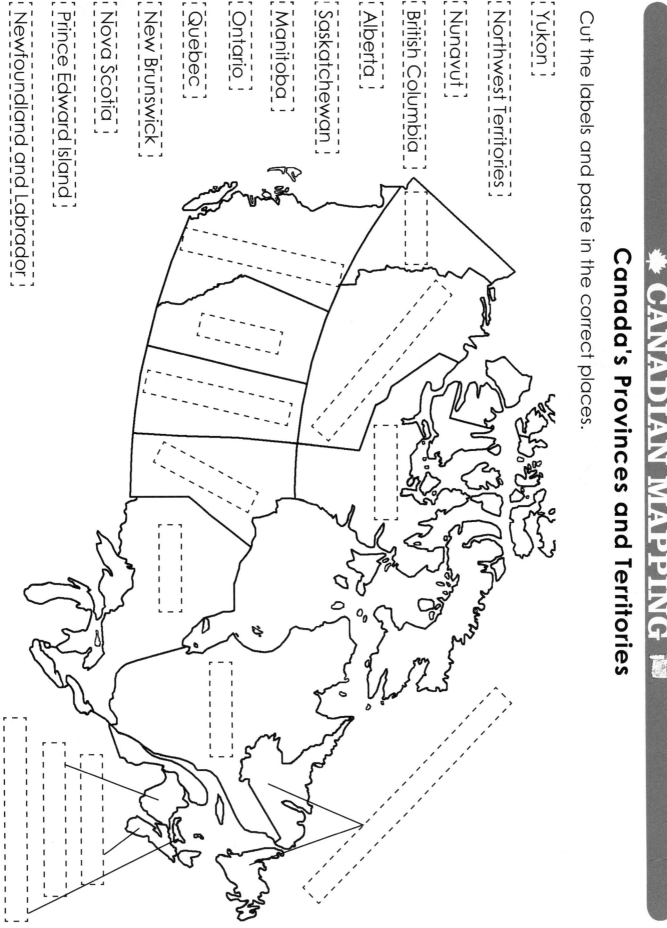

CANADIAN MAPPING

Canada's Provinces and Territories

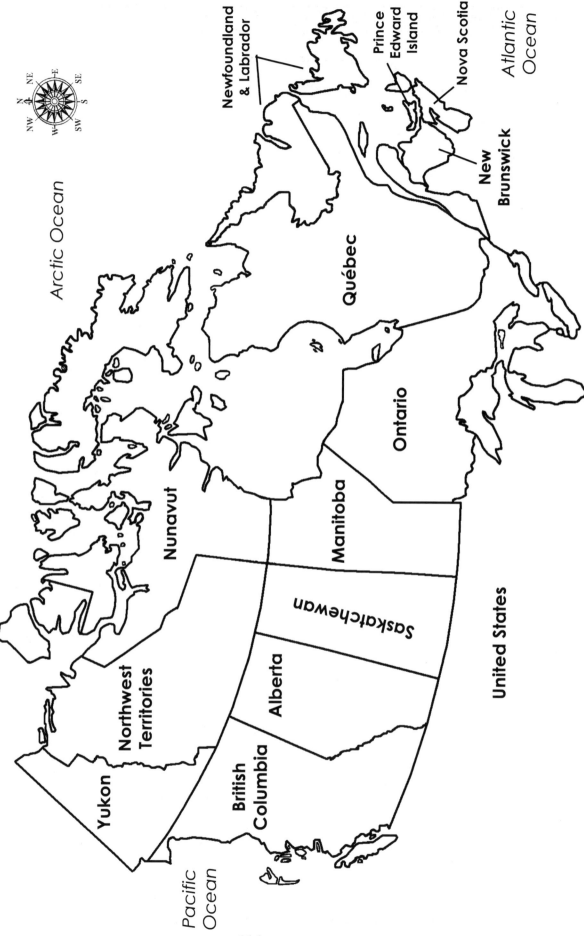

Newfoundland & Labrador

Prince Edward Island

Nova Scotia

Atlantic Ocean

New Brunswick

Arctic Ocean

Québec

Ontario

Nunavut

Manitoba

Saskatchewan

United States

Northwest Territories

Alberta

Yukon

British Columbia

Pacific Ocean

The Names and Shapes of the Provinces and Territories of Canada

Draw lines from these provinces and territories to show where they should be.

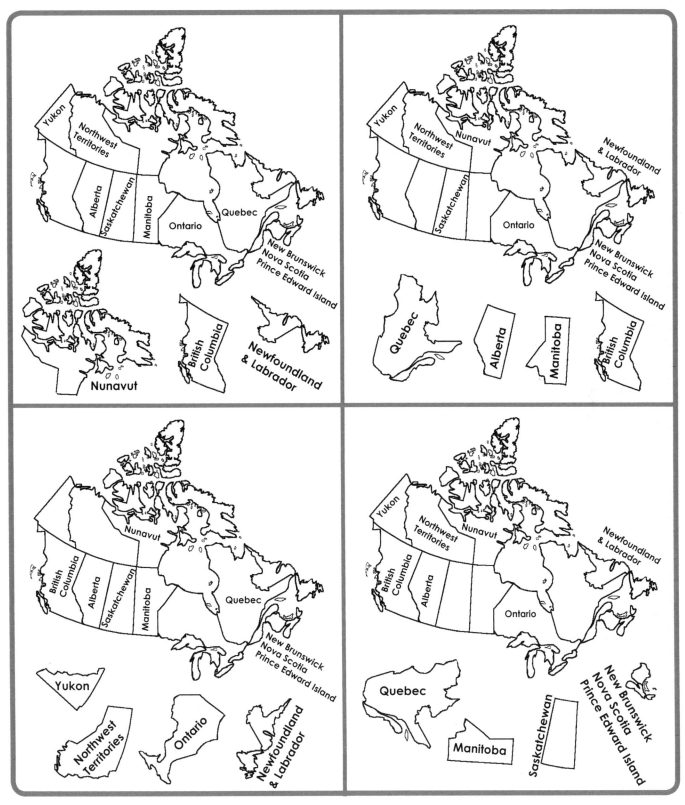

Canada Map Cards

Use these cards for games, activities and assignments.

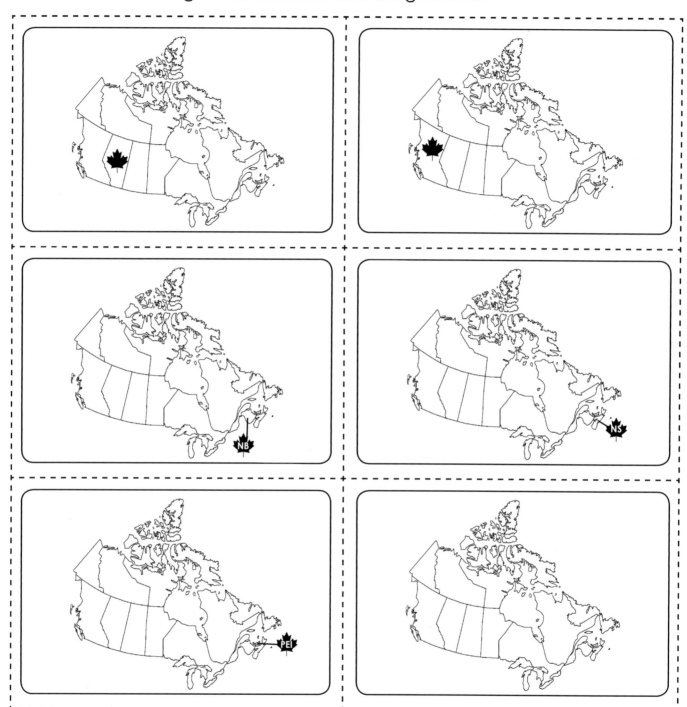

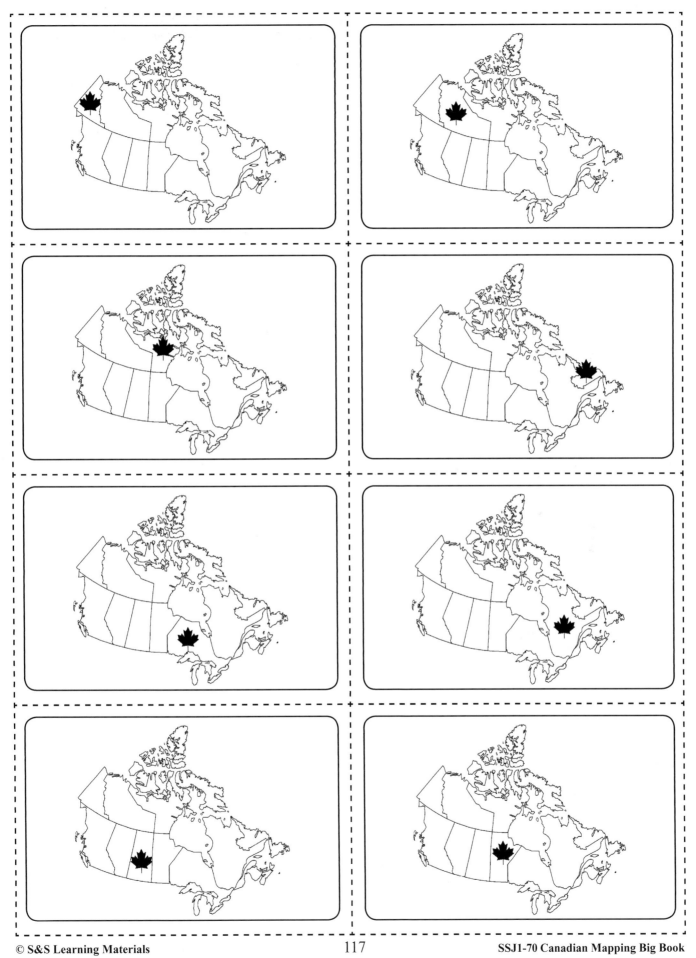

✦ CANADIAN MAPPING 🏳

Canadian Mapping Game Ideas For the Teacher
(For Use With Canada Map Cards)

1. **Twenty Questions:** For each of these variations, attach a province or territory map card to the clothing on the back of each student so that the student does not know what is on the card. On the directive "**Go,**" students will walk about the room, stopping to ask questions one on one. These will be questions with yes/no answers. Students will keep track of how many questions it takes to guess "their" province or territory. The winner guesses correctly, with the least number of questions. Note: it also works well to play this game with one person asking questions of the rest of the class.

Variations:

* All questions must contain a cardinal direction. E.g., "Am I west of Saskatchewan?"

* All questions must contain the name of a large body of water. E.g., "Am I near the Atlantic Ocean?"

* All questions must contain either the word "province" or "territory". E.g., "Am I a territory that is Canada's newest territory?"

2. **Province/Territory Scramble:**

* Distribute 13 map cards to 13 students. (One for each province and territory). On the directive "**Go,**" students will arrange themselves across the front of the room in correct order west to east with their map cards held behind them. (Those with territory cards will stand behind those with province cards.) Students without cards will be asked to name a student and the hidden province/territory based on their knowledge of Canadian maps. E.g., "Ryan-Nova Scotia." (Ryan will then hold his card out front for others to see.) Continue until all provinces and territories are identified.

* Give each student in the class a province/territory card. Students will arrange themselves in scatter formation about the room. The teacher will randomly point to and orally label a corner for each of the following: Maritime Provinces, Prairies, Territories, Near an Ocean, etc. On the directive "**Go,**" students will move safely and quickly to the corner that best matches "their" province or territory. Check the groups at each corner for correct placement. Repeat with different corners and possibly different labels.

3. **Riddle Game:**

* Randomly distribute a map card to each student or pair of students, making sure that others do not see the card. Students will then jot down 5 clues for "their" province or territory. E.g., Volunteers will orally read their clues in riddle format. Others in the class will try to guess after each clue is given.

Variation:

The students write 5 clues for "their" province/territory but one is not correct. While displaying their map card, they read aloud their clues. Others in the class try to guess the incorrect clue based on their knowledge of provinces and territories.

CANADIAN MAPPING

Province and Territory Sort

Yukon	**Y.T.**	Northwest Territories	**N.W.T.**
Nunavut	**NT**	British Columbia	**B.C.**
Alberta	**Alta.**	Saskatchewan	**Sask.**
Manitoba	**Man.**	Ontario	**Ont.**
Quebec	**Que.**	New Brunswick	**N.B.**
Nova Scotia	**N.S.**	Prince Edward Island	**P.E.I.**
Newfoundland and Labrador	**N.L.**		

Print the abbreviations for the provinces and territories in the correct places on the graphic organizer. Some will fit in more than one place.

Borders on the United States	**Ocean Coastline**
_____	_____
_____	_____
_____	_____
Arctic Lands	**The Great Lakes**
_____	_____
_____	_____
_____	_____
Mainly Island(s)	**High Mountains**
_____	_____
_____	_____
_____	_____

Landforms of Canada

Physical maps show the natural features of the earth such as mountains, valleys, ranges, mountains and deserts. These are also called landforms.

1. Draw purple ^^^ in the Rocky Mountains.

2. Draw brown //// in the Interior Plains (prairies).

3. Colour the Arctic Lowlands blue.

4. Draw red ------ in the Hudson Bay Lowlands.

5. Colour the Appalachian Region orange.

6. Colour the Canadian Shield black.

7. Colour the Great Lakes-St. Lawrence Lowlands green.

8. Draw a large dot ● for your community.

9. My community is in _____

(Print the name of the landform for your community.)

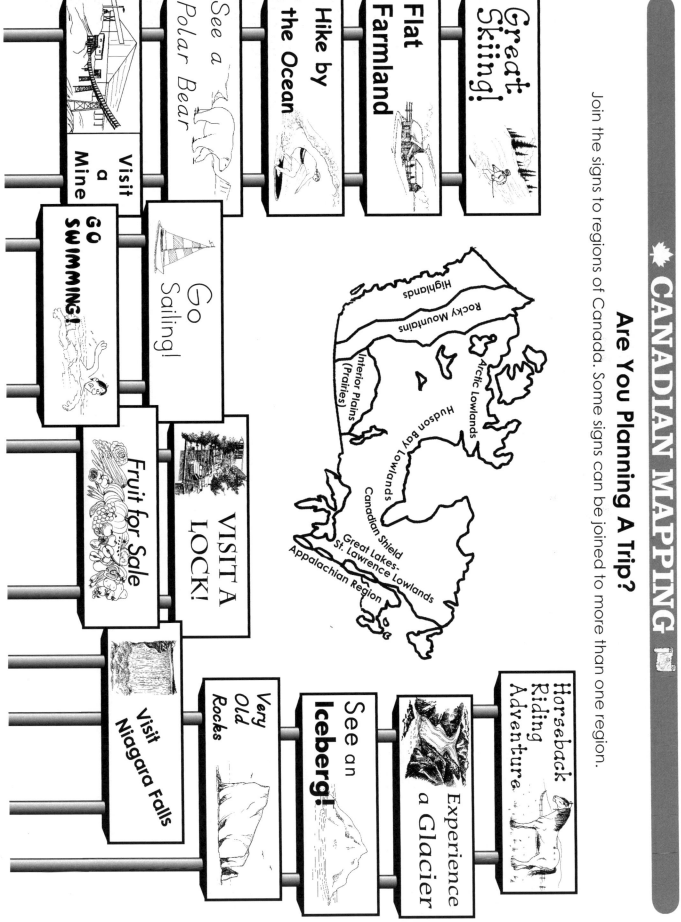

CANADIAN MAPPING

Are You Planning A Trip?

Join the signs to regions of Canada. Some signs can be joined to more than one region.

Great Skiing!

Flat Farmland

Hike by the Ocean

See a Polar Bear

Visit a Mine

GO SWIMMING!

Go Sailing!

Fruit for Sale

VISIT A LOCK!

Visit Niagara Falls

Very Old Rocks

See an Iceberg!

Experience a Glacier

Horseback Riding Adventure

Arctic Lowlands

Rocky Mountains

Highlands

Interior Plains (Prairies)

Hudson Bay Lowlands

Canadian Shield

Great Lakes-St. Lawrence Lowlands

Appalachian Region

★ CANADIAN MAPPING 1

The Oceans

Canada has oceans on three sides. On the map, circle the names of the three oceans.

Pacific Ocean Atlantic Ocean Arctic Ocean

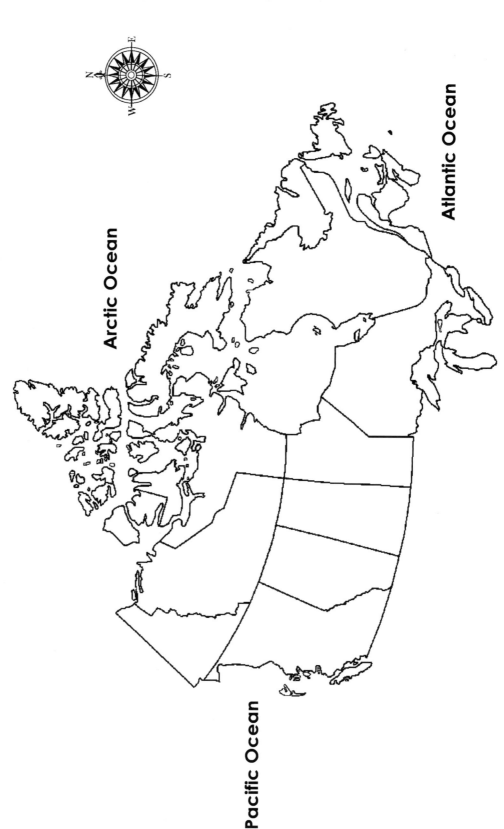

Arctic Ocean

Atlantic Ocean

Pacific Ocean

Did you know that the two red bands of colour on our Canadian flag are for our two oceans Atlantic and Pacific?

Canada's Big Water

1. Draw a line to join the water names below to their correct meaning:

Lake •	• an area of water, smaller than a sea; often surrounded by land
Bay •	• a large body of water, smaller than an ocean
Strait •	• a narrow body of water connecting two larger bodies of water
Ocean •	• a body of fresh or salt water entirely surrounded by land
Sea •	• one of the large areas of the earth into which the water surface is divided
Gulf •	• a part of an ocean, sea or lake extending into land

2. Find your province on the map of Canada. Colour its main bodies of water blue.

3. Add words to this chart. (Use the map to help you.)

Ocean	Lake	Bay	Strait	Sea	Gulf
Atlantic					

Be a Water Detective!

Find the water by using the clues below. Fill in the blanks with the correct water names.

1. James _____
2. Great Slave _____
3. Labrador _____
4. Lake _____
5. Davis _____

6. Lake_____
7. Baffin_____
8. Gulf of _____
9. Beaufort_____
10. Pacific_____

Your teacher will help you to find your community on the map of Canada. Print the name of a body of water from the above list on the spaces below.

I live nearest _____

I live far away from _____

Ontario's Big Water

Ontario has many lakes and rivers. Many cities and towns have developed along the waterways. Use crayons to do the following:

1. Outline the coasts of the 4 Great Lakes that touch Ontario-----dark blue

2. Outline the coastline of Hudson Bay and James Bay --------------green

3. Outline the coast of Georgian Bay--orange

4. Draw an arrow ⇨ to point at the Ontario part of the St. Lawrence River.

5. Trace other rivers--light blue

Print the names of six big cities that are on the major waterways in Ontario:

1._____   4. _____

2._____   5. _____

3._____   6. _____

Ontario's Landforms

Physical Map of Ontario   **Satellite Image of Ontario**

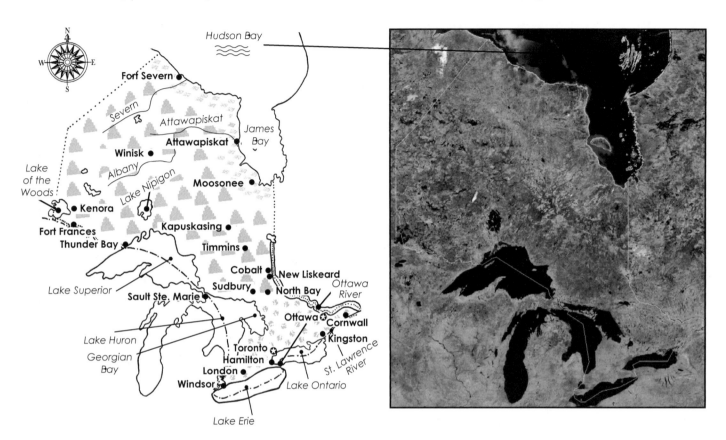

1. Draw straight lines (use a ruler to help you) from the map to the satellite image. Join matching places. A sample has been done for you.

2. Sort items from the map onto this organizer:

Landform Regions	Cities	Rivers	Lakes
Hudson Bay Lowlands			
Canadian Shield			
Great Lakes St. Lawrence Lowlands			

126   SSJ1-70 Canadian Mapping Big Book

Landforms of British Columbia

Physical Map of British Columbia   **Satellite Image of British Columbia**

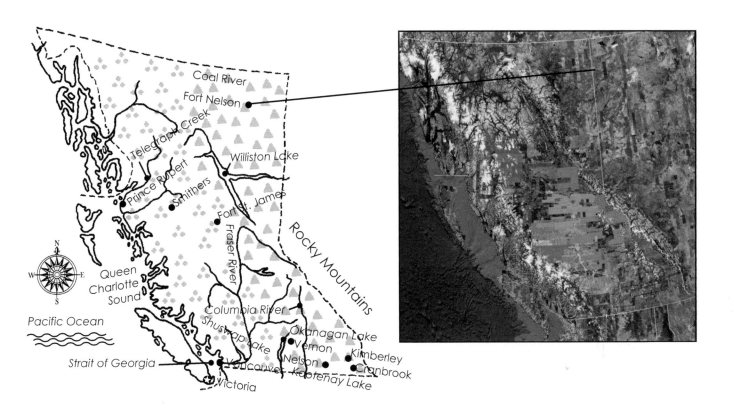

1. Draw straight lines (use a ruler to help you) from the map to the satellite image. Join matching places. A sample has been done for you. Join as many as you can.

2. Sort items from the map onto this organizer:

Landform Regions	Cities	Rivers	Lakes
∴ Highlands			
▲ Rocky Mountains			

☀ CANADIAN MAPPING 🗺

Comparing Two Provinces

Use the physical maps and satellite images of British Columbia and Ontario to compare these provinces. Cut the labels given below and paste them onto the organizer in the correct locations.

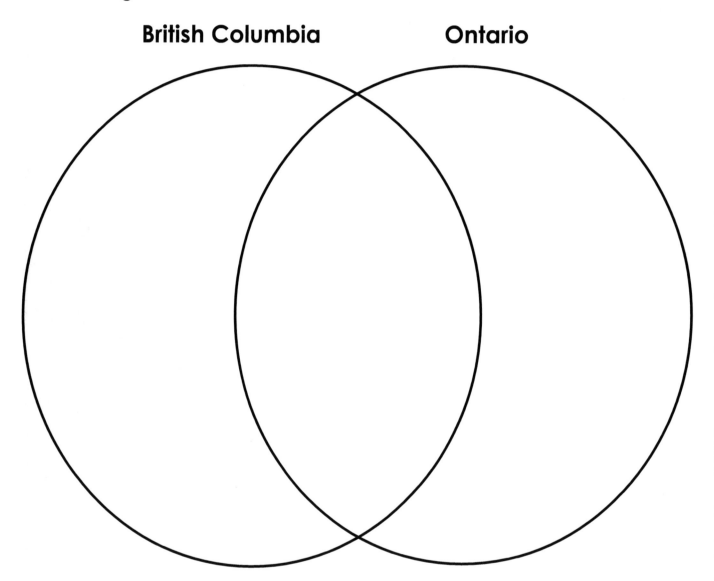

British Columbia   Ontario

mountain skiing	many big cities	central	travel locations
ocean fishing	farmland	ocean	many islands
huge freshwater lakes	flatter land near Hudson Bay	many inland lakes	west
logging	rocky shield	mining	central
very few towns	Rocky Mountains	scenic views	factories

CANADIAN MAPPING

Physical Map of Canada

Physical maps show the natural features of the earth, such as mountains, valleys, flat lands and deserts. These are called landforms.

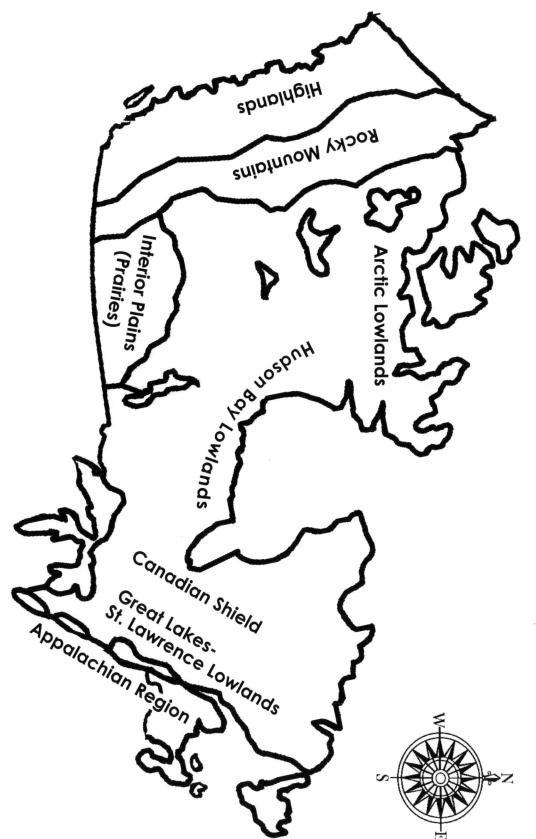

© S&S Learning Materials

129

SSJ1-70 Canadian Mapping Big Book

✿ CANADIAN MAPPING 📜

My Canadian Community

On the physical map of Canada, draw a big dot ● to show where you live. The physical map of Canada can tell us many things about our community.

Circle the statements that tell about your community:

in the mountains   in the flat land

near a Great Lake   near an ocean

near the Arctic   in the Canadian Shield

near the St. Lawrence River   on an island

On the physical map of Canada, do the following:

1. Colour the physical area where you live brown.

2. Colour the lakes and rivers blue.

Use the physical map to tell the following:

1. I live (circle one) **West East** of the Rocky Mountains.

2. I live (circle one) **South North East West** of the prairies.

3. I live near a big lake.

4. I live in the landform area called _____

Urban and Rural Communities - 1

Draw a line to join the following words to the correct picture.
Some words will be joined to both pictures.

Rural

A rural area is a country setting,
usually with many farms.

Urban

An urban area is a city or town with
many buildings and streets.

Transportation

transport truck

tractor

taxi cabs

major highways

truck carrying livestock

subway

Buildings

factories

groups of many houses

barns

houses with fields
around them

high rise buildings

churches

Land Use

farms

cattle

industrial
developments

many houses built
on fields

shopping malls

greenhouses on fields

Urban and Rural Communities – 2

Rural

A rural area is a country setting, usually with many farms. This is a map of a rural area in Canada.

Urban

An urban area is a city or town with many buildings and streets. This is a map of an urban area in Canada.

Cut the pictures and paste them onto the map in the correct places.

- -

A Car Trip in Canada

Cut out the car. Use it to "take a car trip" across Canada. Start in Whitehorse, Yukon. Use a pencil to trace around the car at each stop. Label the car you draw at each stop **U** for Urban or **R** for rural. Make at least 6 stops, 3 urban and 3 rural. End your trip in St. John's Newfoundland and Labrador.

Assessment One – Canadian Mapping

Students will need a pencil, a set of crayons and a sheet with a large map of Canada with provinces, territories and major cities labelled. It should also have a compass rose and a Legend/Key. Teachers: Distribute one map to each student in your group. Read aloud each direction. Repeat as required, allowing the appropriate time for completion. Start by asking students to put their names and today's date on the sheet.

Name: _____ **Date:** _____

1. Trace the outline shape of Canada red. ☐

2. Put a big red C on Canada. ☐

3. Colour our privince (territory) light green. ☐

4. Circle the symbols in the Legend/Key with a purple crayon. ☐

5. On the map, draw a big star symbol where your community is located. ☐

6. Look for the great lakes. Colour them blue. ☐

7. Draw a big P on the Pacific Ocean. ☐

8. Put a big A on the Atlantic Ocean. ☐

9. Circle any urban community. ☐

10. Draw a big R in any rural area. ☐

For the teacher

Total ____

✦ CANADIAN MAPPING 📜

Assessment Two – Canadian Mapping

Students will need a pencil, a set of crayons and a sheet with a large map of Canada with provinces, territories and major cities labelled. It should also have a compass rose, a Legend/Key, the three major parallels of latitude (50N, 60N and 70N) on it. Teachers: Distribute one map to each student in your group. Read aloud each direction. Repeat as required, allowing the appropriate time for completion. Start by asking students to put their names and today's date on the sheet.

Name: _____   **Date:** _____

1. On the map, draw a big star symbol where your community is located. ☐

2. Trace the parallels of latitude purple. ☐

3. Circle a city near the 50N parallel of latitude. ☐

4. Underline the name of the city that is NE of Toronto. ☐

5. Put a rectangle around the name of the territory that is NW of Alberta. ☐

6. Circle the name of a city that is SW of Edmonton. ☐

7. Draw several brown ∧'s where we find the Rocky Mountains. ☐

8. Use the Legend/Key to help you. Join any one of the symbols on it to the same symbol on the map. ☐

9. Print a large A where we find the Arctic Ocean. ☐

10. Print HB on Hudson Bay. ☐

For the teacher   Total ____

Answer Key

Canada Sort *(Page 87)*
1. Canada: Northern Hemisphere, North of the Equator, Near North Pole, Western Hemisphere 1. Equator – hot
2. South Pole – cold 3. North Pole – cold

Eastern Hemisphere

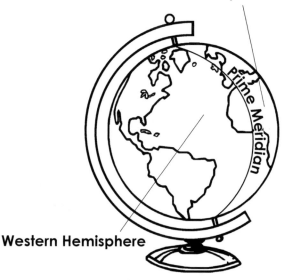

Western Hemisphere

Compare Two Provinces – Using Symbols *(Page 93)*
Ontario
1. Capital City – Toronto 2. Two other Cities – Ottawa and Hamilton 3. National Capital – Yes 4. Ontario is part of - Canada 5. Largest body of water - Hudson Bay 6. A nearby country – United States

Saskatchewan
1. Capital City – Regina 2. Two other cities – Saskatoon and Prince Albert 3. National Capital – No 4. Saskatchewan is part of – Canada 5. Largest body of water – Lake Athabasca 6. A nearby country – United States

Compare Two Territories – Using Symbols *(Page 94)*
1. Capital City – Whitehorse 2. Two other cities – Dawson and Watson Lake 3. Many islands – No 4. Yukon is part of - Canada 5. Smallest territory – Yes 6. A nearby country – United States
1. Capital city – Iqaluit 2. Two other cities – Rankin Inlet and Arviat 3. Many islands – Yes 4. Nunavut is part of – Canada. 5. Largest territory – Yes 6. A nearby country - Greenland

Map of Ontario – Measuring Distance *(page 101)*
Hamilton to Moosonee – 900 km, London to Toronto –150 km, Ottawa to Sault Ste Marie – 700 km, Toronto to Windsor – 350 km

Map of Quebec and Labrador *(page 102)*
Montreal, Quebec to St. John's, Newfoundland 1600 km, Laval, Quebec to Havre Saint Pierre, Quebec 1000 km, Quebec, Quebec to Montreal, Quebec 250 km, Val-d'or, Quebec to Montreal, Quebec 600 km

Canada's Funland –Using Scale on a Map (Page 103)

1. 10m 2. 10m 3. 10m 4. 20m 5. 20m
6. 15m 7. 15m 8. 50m 9. 150m

Parallels of Latitude (Page 104)

1. Winnipeg 2. 50° N 3. 60°N and 70°N 4. Whitehorse

Up and Down -Introducing Longitude (Page 107)

1. Prime Meridian 2. West 3. East

Meridians –Using Meridians of Longitude (Page 108)

1. Vancouver 2. Winnipeg 3. Ottawa and Montreal 4. 115 degrees 5. St. John's
6. 105 degrees

Mapping Canada (Page 111)

Canada Physical: Use to see where the mountains are located
Aerial Photo: Use to see the way roads are arranged
Satellite Image: Use to see what weather is coming to an area
Canada Political: Use to see all of Canada's provinces and territories

More Mapping Canada (Page 112)

Canada Physical: Use this map to see where very flat farmland is found
Road Map: Use this map when searching for something
Satellite Image: Use this map to see if the weather is good for flying an airplane
Canada Political: Use this map to see the shapes of the provinces and territories

Province and Territory Sort (Page 119)

Borders on the United States: B.C., Alta., Sask., Man., Ont., Que., N.B.
Arctic Lands: Y.T., N.W.T., NT, Que.
Mainly Islands: NT. P.E.I., N.L.
Ocean Coastline: B.C., N.S., N.B., Que., P.E.I., N.L., Y.T., N.W.T., NT
The Great Lakes: Ont.
High Mountains: B.C., Alta.

Canada's Big Water: (Page 123)

Bay: a part of an ocean sea or lake extending into land
Strait: a narrow body of water connecting two larger bodies of water
Ocean: one of the large areas of the earth into which the water surface is divided
Sea: a large body of water, smaller than an ocean
Gulf: an area of water smaller than a sea; often surrounded by land

Be a Water Detective (Page 124)

1. James Bay 2. Great Slave Lake
3. Labrador Sea 4. Lake (various)
5. Davis Strait 6. Lake (various)
7. Baffin Bay 8. Gulf of St. Lawrence
9. Beaufort Sea 10. Pacific Ocean

Comparing Two Provinces (Page 128)

British Columbia: mountain skiing, Ocean fishing, Very few towns, Rocky Mountains, many islands, west

logging, farmland, ocean, mining, scenic views, travel locations

Ontario: Huge freshwater lakes, many big cities, flatter land near Hudson Bay, rocky shield, many inland lakes, central

Urban and Rural Communities – 2 (Page 132)

Rural   Urban

Map of British Columbia

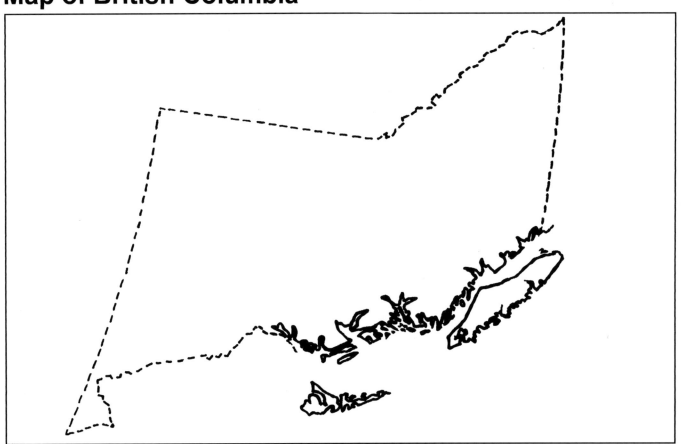

Map of Alberta

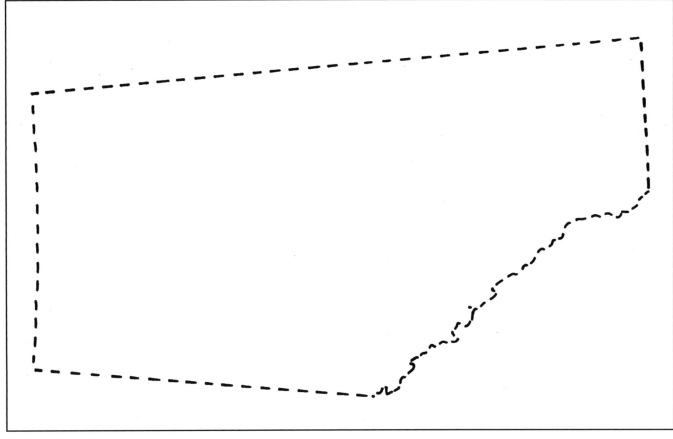

Map of Saskatchewan

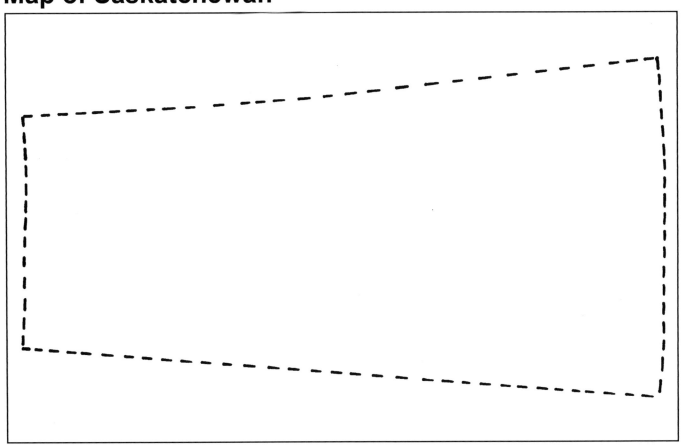

Map of Manitoba

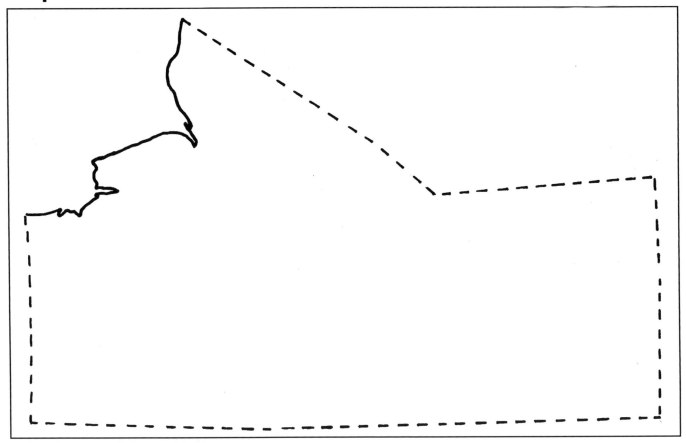

Map of Ontario

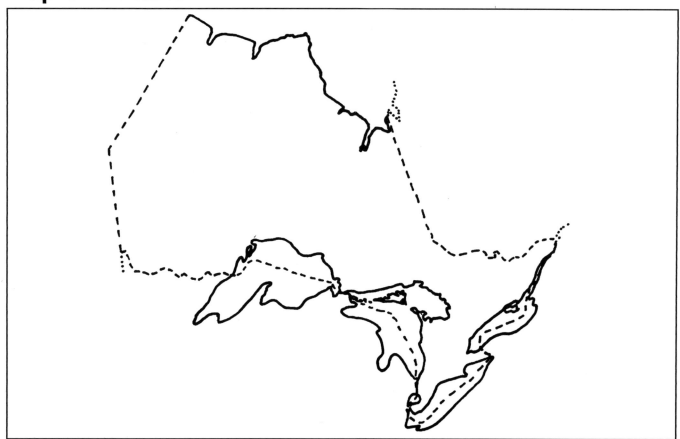

Map of Quebec

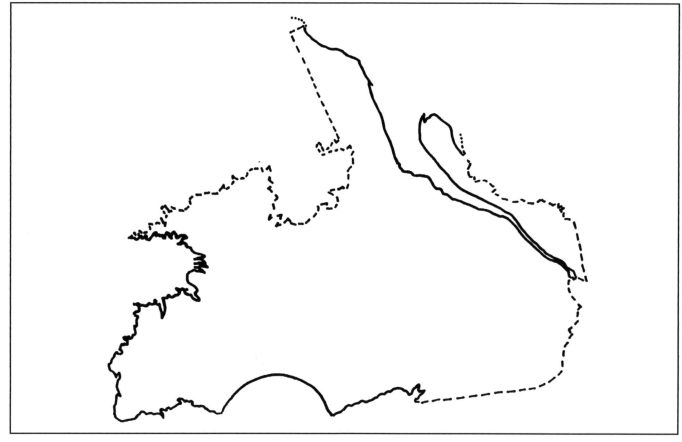

Map of Nova Scotia

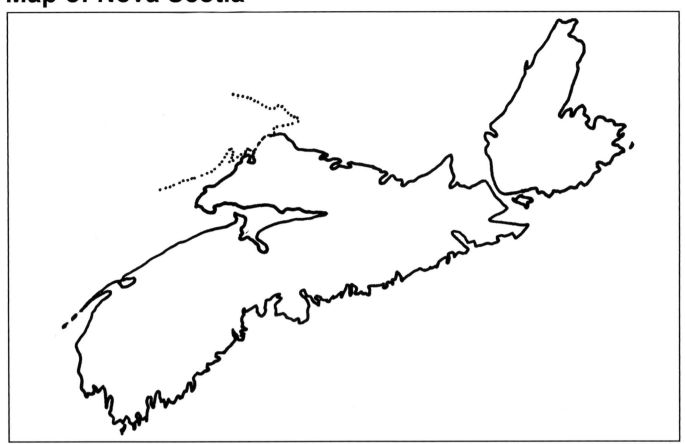

Map of New Brunswick

Map of Newfoundland & Labrador

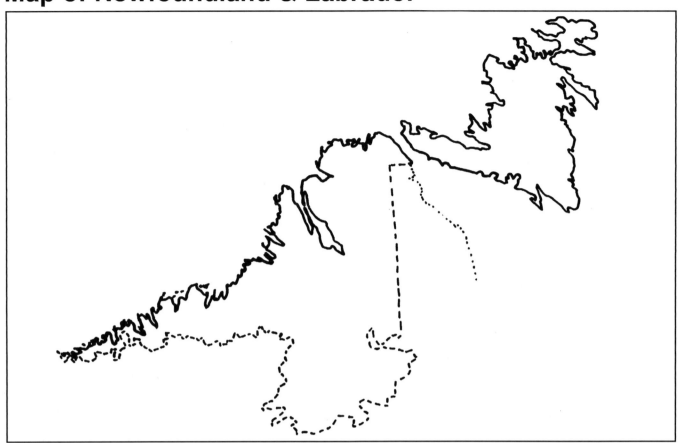

Map of Prince Edward Island

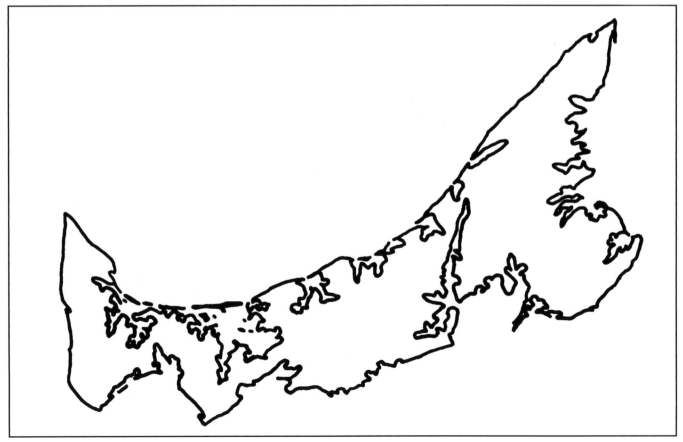

Map of Northwest Territories

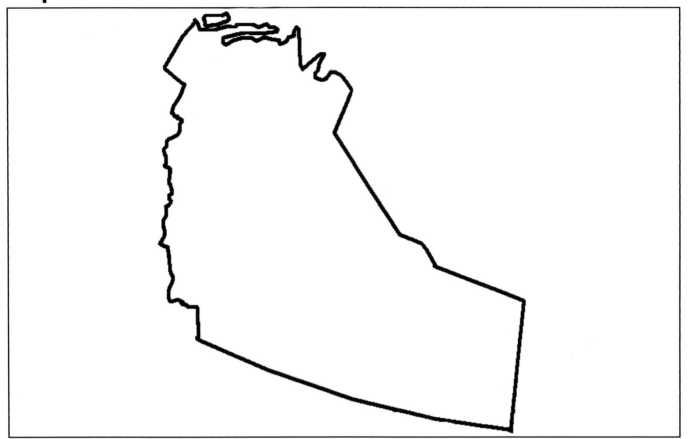

Map of Yukon Territory

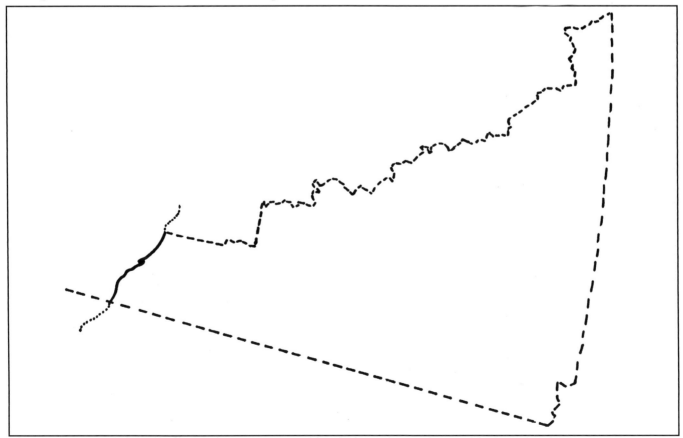

Map of Nunavut

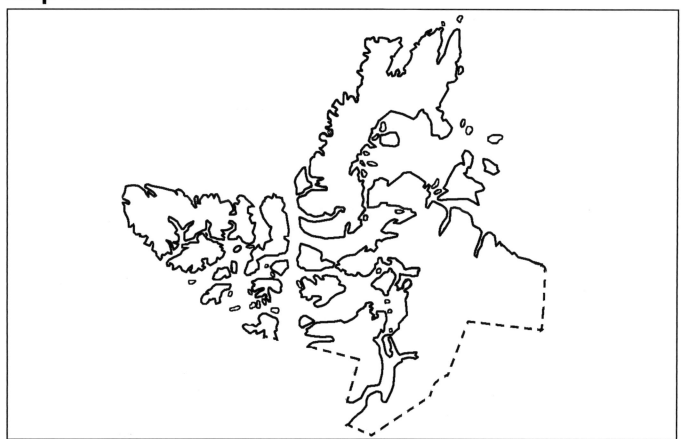

Map of Canada

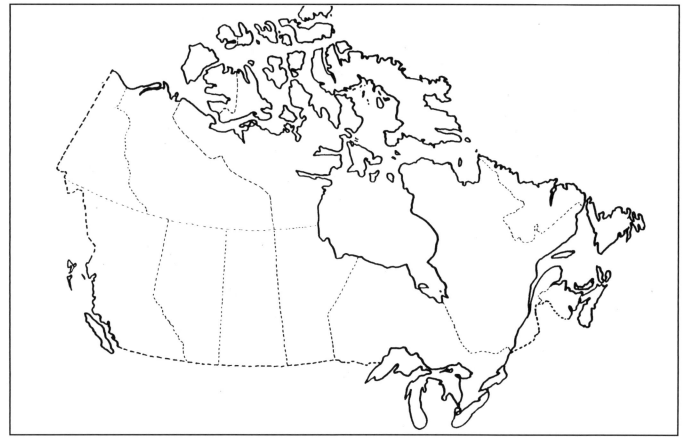

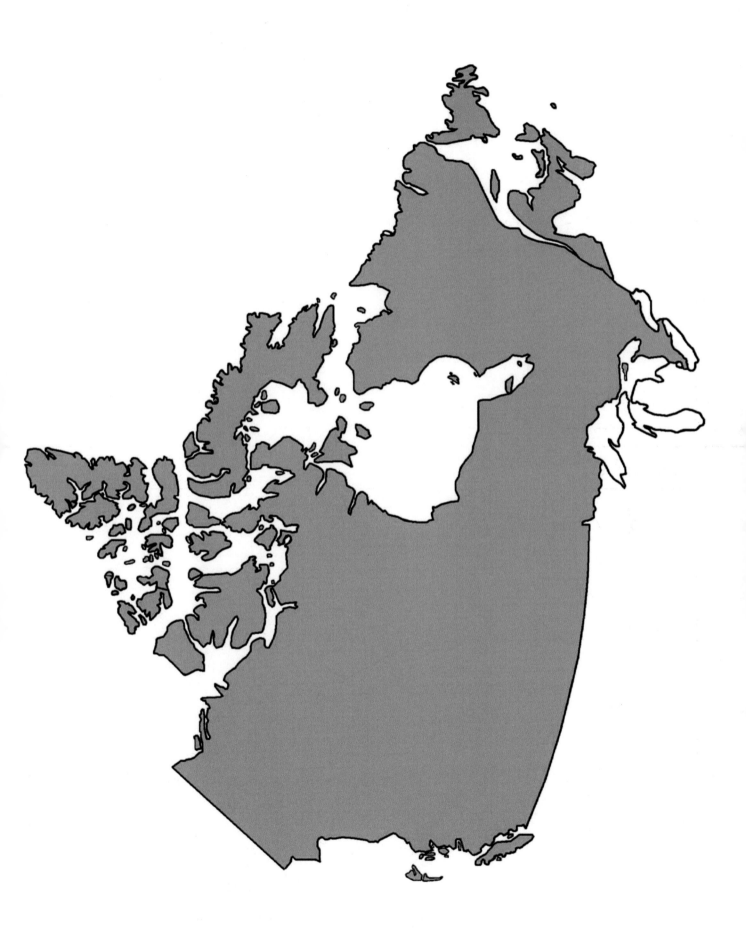

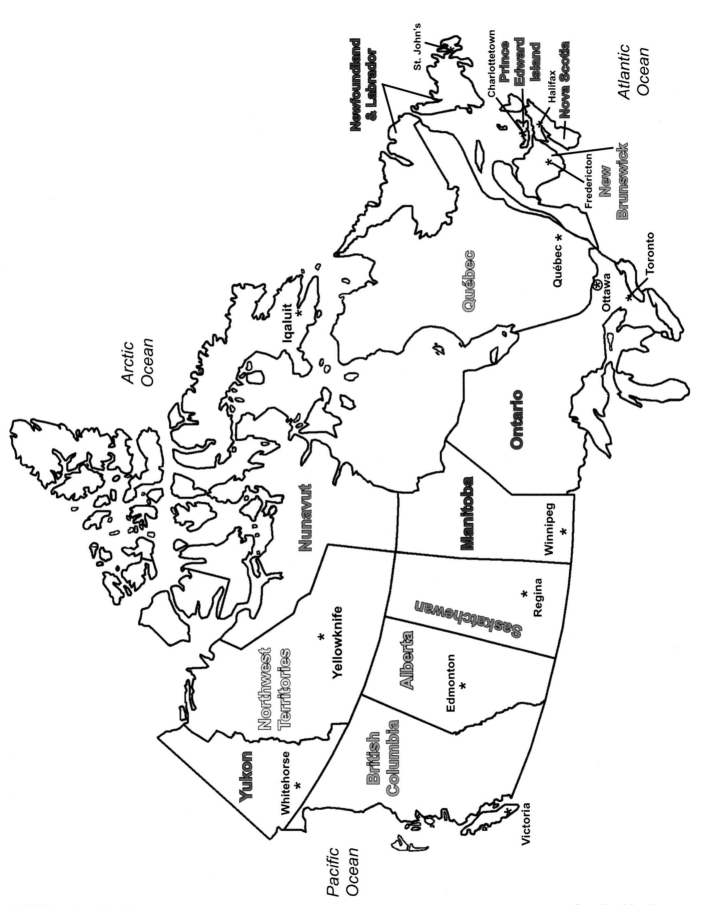

Newfoundland & Labrador

St. John's

Charlottetown
Prince Edward Island

Halifax
Nova Scotia

Fredericton
New Brunswick

Atlantic Ocean

Toronto

Québec *

Québec

Ottawa ⊛

*

Ontario

Iqaluit
*

Arctic Ocean

Nunavut

Manitoba

Winnipeg
*

Regina
*

Saskatchewan

Yellowknife
*

Northwest Territories

Alberta

Edmonton
*

British Columbia

Yukon

Whitehorse
*

Victoria
*

Pacific Ocean

Canadian Mapping

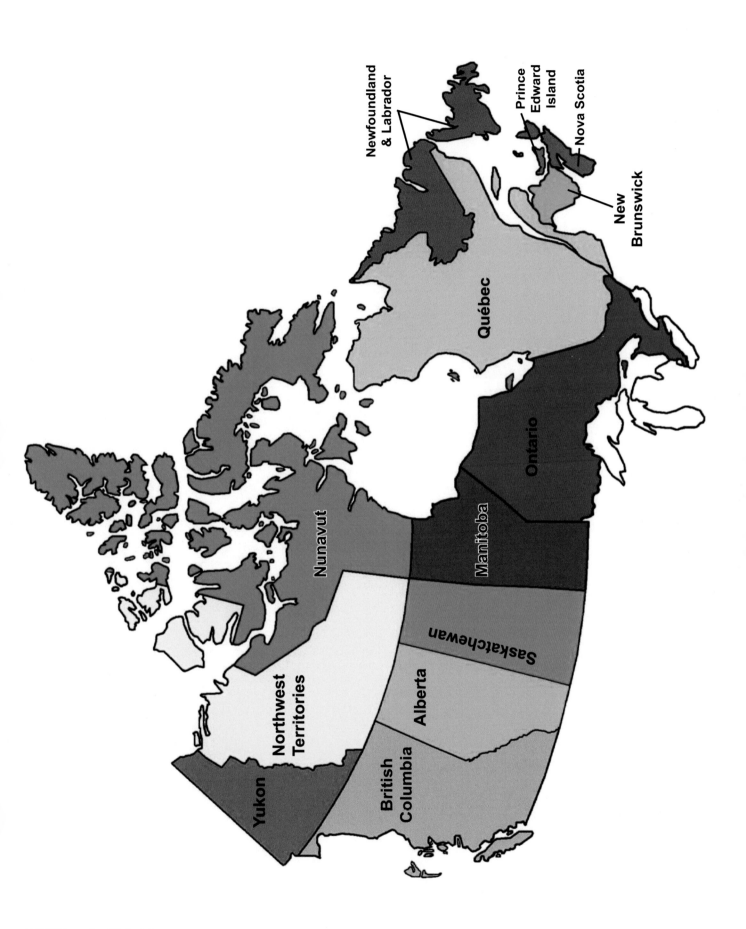

Newfoundland & Labrador

Prince Edward Island

Nova Scotia

New Brunswick

Québec

Ontario

Manitoba

Nunavut

Saskatchewan

Alberta

Northwest Territories

British Columbia

Yukon

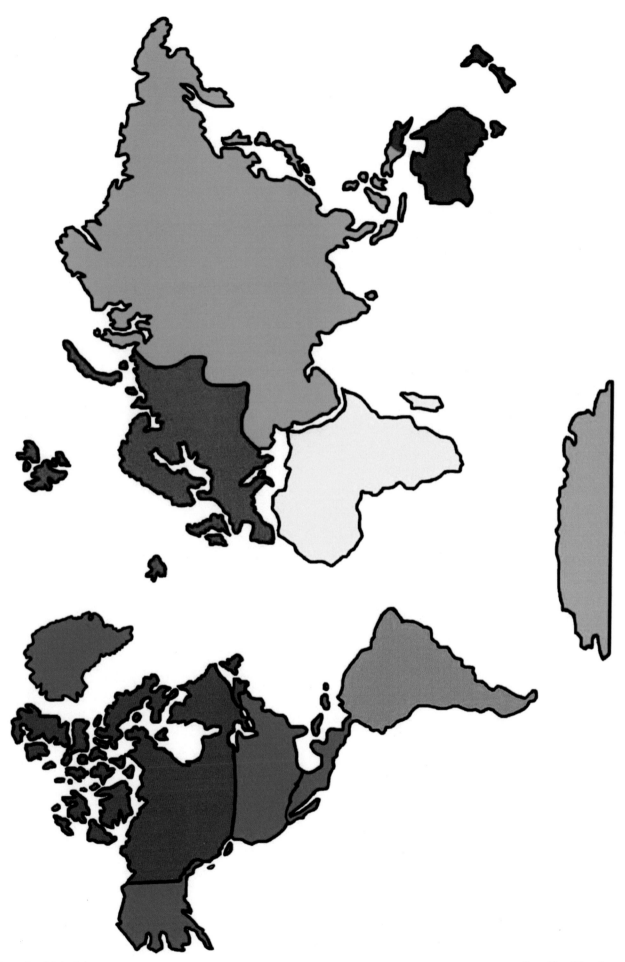